Passages – Transitions – Intersections

Volume 5

General Editors:

Paola Partenza (University of Chieti-Pescara, Italy)

Andrea Mariani (University of Chieti-Pescara, Italy)

Paola Partenza (ed.)

Sin's Multifaceted Aspects in Literary Texts

This is a peer-reviewed volume.

V&R unipress

Bibliographic information published by the Deutsche Nationalbibliothek

The Deutsche Nationalbibliothek lists this publication in the Deutsche Nationalbibliografie; detailed bibliographic data are available online: http://dnb.d-nb.de.

ISSN 2365-9173
ISBN 978-3-8471-0852-8

You can find alternative editions of this book and additional material on our website: www.v-r.de

This volume is published thanks to the F. A. R. S. funds of the Department of Modern Languages, Literatures and Cultures, University "G. d'Annunzio", Chieti-Pescara.

Contents

Acknowledgements

This volume is the result of an international research project started in 2016, which has involved distinguished scholars from different Universities. I am especially grateful to those with whom I have realised it, as well as the anonymous reader that contributed greatly to the development of this volume. For its defects and eccentricities, s/he is, of course, blameless. Further, I would like to thank the colleagues of the Department of Modern Languages, Literatures and Cultures, who have supported the publication of this volume.

Paola Partenza

Introduction: The Concept of Sin in British, French, and American Literary Texts from XVI to XIX Century

Within art, society culture, philosophy, literature and many other spheres, a constant issue being dealt with is that of sin. Reappraisal and reevaluation of this concept have proceeded down varied stimulating paths in relation to the multidisciplinary appraisal, although philosophical aesthetic and epistemic emphases commonly reflect issues present in literature. It is apparent that many define sin as the contravention of religious law, an activity considered as extremely shameful and a fault against widely accepted moral or religious principles, as a traditional conception of sin.

Philosophical treatises and literature have regularly drawn on the notion of sin. In *Macbeth* (Act IV, Scene III), Malcolm emphasises sins of all form such as deception, viciousness, greed and excess, in a memorable scene. In Act I, Scene III of *Richard III*, Queen Margaret comments that every manifestation of hell, death and sin are represented in the character. In Chapter Five, Section 5.4 of *Vindication of the Rights of Women*, Mary Wollstonecraft suggests that prejudice – regardless of whether being a pervasively held position – as underpinning power held by despots, is their original sin and undoubtedly a fundamental pillar of their control, as well as being considered one of man's entitlements; in terms of women's conduct, Wollstonecraft condemned the majority of authors for taking the same approach and perspective. Many literary or philosophical works discuss the concept of sin. For example, the "mortal sin" is referred to in *Childe Harold's Pilgrimage* by Lord Byron; in Chapter Two of Elizabeth Gaskell's *Wives and Daughters*, a "sensitive girl" considers herself a "miserable sinner", in *Prometheus Bound* where it is said "a sinner suffers his sin's penalty". In *Beyond Good and Evil*, Friedrich Nietzsche suggested that the notions of God and sin, which are solemnly upheld yet are responsible for much violence and pain in the world, may in future be perceived as an elderly person sees a child's toy and his pain, although "perhaps 'the old man' will then need another toy and another pain – still enough of a child, an eternal child!". Thus, sin has been a pervasive subject in all kinds of works.

In certain instances, texts clearly refer to sin, while in other it is more of an ambiguous and obscured notion. While rational and atheist characters' principles and questions surrounding their redemption may be emphasised, in other works it is those adhering to traditional moral values which are emphasised. Significantly, philosophical, poetic and novelistic works have continuously adopted sin as a subject, regardless of the multifarious nature of its analysis that is evident if we consider it across various kinds of art and literature. Contemporarily, our existing knowledge suggested we should reassess the notion of sin and human associations with it, irrespective of sin's utilisation and manipulation as a concept, the extent to which we refuse the original sin, our beliefs about the restrictions it places on us, the chances it offers to oppose the bias and errors in male-dominated society, or our view of it as a religious transgression or guilt. We should consider how the constantly altering and dynamic nature of our environment, as well as our perspectives of it, have also shaped philosophical, poetic and novelistic reactions. Alongside the established understanding of sin, discourse, poetry and novels have responded to *sin* variously, due to the blossoming of ideas. With human history being constantly punctuated by the notion of sin, assessing writers' responses and exploration of the subject is the basis of this study. French, American and British literature's responses to the notion of sin will be investigated through studies included in this volume. The objective is to analyse how the broad reaction and reassessment of sin has been intersected by multifarious constructs, such as redemption, the original sin and guilt.

Igor Djordjevic, in the first chapter of the volume, explores how polemics and poetry were pervaded with an essentially religious conception of sin during the Early Modern era, which saw both religious reformation and struggle. Nevertheless, subversion, betrayal, revolt and regicide also emerged as acknowledged sins in the political realm. While English monarchs' crimes against their own people, in terms of politically sinful tyranny, ran through the informal discussions among the people as well as their cultural and historical recollections, any criticism or action against the sovereign by the subject was denounced as a sin in the official Elizabethan discourse. As represented in literature, the latter official discourse is exemplified in Mirrors for Princes, indeed in the *Faerie Queene* by Spenser, whereas the former position is laid bare against the Elizabethan era's standards through Shakespeare's presentation of the political misdeeds and sins of monarchs in his plays dealing with the War of the Roses. In Elizabethan England, the popular reputations of King Henry VI and Richard II were two of the lowest among monarchs; Shakespeare's portrayal of these kings is explored in this chapter, as well as how the recovery of their reputations may proceed from the dramatized, poetic portrayals of their failed sovereignty. The topos of sacrificial monarch is utilised by Shakespeare, resulting in the viewer reacting to their deaths in an alternative manner to that of a consumer of contemporaneous chronicler's accounts, although Shakespeare drew heavily on these. The most harrowing periods within collective cultural recollection may be channelled through the sacrificial monarch motif. For example, comparable redemptive aims were sought through an almost indistinguishable collection of motifs relating to Charles I, the sacrificial King of *Eikon Basilike*, which contributed significantly to a rehabilitation of the monarch following his execution. Ultimately, England's collective memory has a structure of sorrow, in which the last moments and ultimate death of sacrificial monarchs such as Charles contribute to constructing it, as Marvell has suggested.

In her assessment of the culture of the Restoration period, Margarete Rubik appraises how the passionate adoption of the libertine character challenged the Commonwealth era's religious fervour. Thus, established Christian thought was targeted by the liberalised philosophers and writers of the period in order to stoke its ire, with a sacrilegious and mocking approach. One example where religious terminology was adopted in order to confront and defy in a blasphemous manner, removed from its sacred context, is in Aphra Behn's (1640–1689) corpus, where the word *sin* is adopted with unexpected regularity. Whether prostitution, infidelity or general coarseness, sexual acts are almost inevitably being referred to when Behn uses the terms sinner or sin. Indeed, moral ambiguity is sometimes apparent with regard to sinning, typically when a woman is confidentially engaged to a man and yet she is compelled to marry another, providing semi-moral appropriateness for her fiancé to continue their relationship while she resides in a sham, loveless marriage. Regardless, the belief that the sovereign power and legal institutions defined what is sinful for their own ends, with moral relativism and natural urges dominating humans in a Hobbesian state of nature, was often the only reason that caddish individuals needed, rather than identifying moral loopholes.

The presentation of women cads, shorn of any scruples or feelings of ethical responsibility associated with their quest for sexual gratification, was sometimes engaged in by Behn. Furthermore, she portrayed male libertines as sexually appealing figures, despite their misogynistic character. It is also apparent that pragmatism, as opposed to religiosity, is the reason for other females resisting the pursuit of sexual pleasure. Therefore, it is a particular unequal cultural standard for women, as opposed to a godly directive, that drove virginal expectations. Rather than death or criminal sanctions, it is alienation from society that results from female transgression. For Behn, an initial stage of human innocence, prior to human comprehension of sin that developed through the Christian commandments' authoritarian nature, was a Golden era exemplified by the Carib people's idyllic religious and law-free society celebrated in *Oroonoko*. Moreover, Behn approved of the revenge taken by masculine, youthful cavaliers and the figurative triumph of royalist principles, in their affairs with Whig wives whose husbands opposed the Stuarts. Thus, Behn's characters draw on absurd statements, extreme ethical principles, ludicrous semi-constructed arguments in order to ridicule sin. It is proposed that free love is a form of benevolence, whereas the unreachability of a high-class woman is the real sin, to take as one example. However, when such women are ultimately won by the male character, the cad inevitably seeks a different lover, conveying the actual Hobbesian and insincere misogynistic discourse and the emptiness of rhetoric. Therefore, the political and religious environment of Restoration period is explored to situate Behn's representation of guilt and sin in Rubik's essay.

John F. Maune's chapter is concerned with the protagonist of *Coriolanus*, one of Shakespeare's later tragedies. Coriolanus was exemplary of Roman morality, inculcated by Volumnia Coriolanus' mother, in accordance with the Ten Commandments and Roman societal norms. Coriolanus' pride – one of the seven deadly sins – has been emphasised by the majority of academics and indeed, the plebeians of Rome. His disdain for ordinary citizens, military capability and noble family line were all sources of his pride. Coriolanus' considerable naivety – bereft of skills of shrewdness or political intrigue despite being a noble soldier – was how Shakespeare characterised him. Even so, Coriolanus ultimately pursues vengeance against Rome, after the plebeians, guided by the tribunes, end their backing of Coriolanus' moves to become consul. Therefore, wrath, a further deadly sin, indeed characterises Coriolanus' actions. His dominant power and strength may easily be brought to bear against his enemies in Rome by the intercession scene, marking his transition to having a god-like status. However, he leaves Rome untouched after his mother's imploring, positing him as more of a Jesus figure than the god Mars – a commonly made comparison. In doing so, his mother's inculcated principles are shed by Coriolanus. In order to forgive his enemies, he risks his own wellbeing and foregoes the wrath of the supreme warrior. Thus, Maune argues that Coriolanus' actions reflect those of Jesus Christ, the epitome of peace in Christian thought, with Mars' (god of war) tenets and Roman principles instilled since birth rejected by the protagonist; it is not pride but wrath that Coriolanus is characterised by for a time.

The moral quandary underpinning *Heart of Darkness*, Joseph Conrad's mysterious work, is explored through the Freudian notion of guilt in Ibrahim A. El-Hussari's chapter. The British protagonist and seaman, Charlie Marlow, a seemingly virtuous individual, is the emphasis of El-Hussari's exploration. Kurtz, the main representative of the European Ivory Corporation, has ceased exporting ivory to Europe, with Kurtz presumptively declared as lost to the Congolese Jungle; Marlow is assigned to travel to Africa and report on Kurtz's status. As Marlow seeks to find Kurtz while traveling along the River Congo, the magnitude of man's evil is slowly revealed to him. Ultimately, he delves to his deepest depth of moral revelation and understanding of his own soul upon arriving at the limits of the navigable jungle, the gloomiest location. At this point,

Kurtz's body has failed and he has surrendered to the jungle's sinister dynamics, proving to be a fallen idol for Marlow. A fading Kurtz reveals the reality of his activities in Africa in hushed tones to Marlow, who is the sole individual present at Kurtz's admission and also the internal reporter of the story. In the jungle's depths, Marlow believes that Kurtz is a mirror of himself, with this unification of the Europeans through their guilt marking the precise point where Freud's analysis becomes relevant. Indicative of this is Marlow's decision to save himself and return home. Here, Marlow is reluctant to relate Kurtz's fate, or reveal the nature of European colonialism, despite the pressures on him to do so. When Marlow travels to meet Kurtz's betrothed, the "intended", to pass on his con- dolences one year later, Kurtz's final words are not related truthfully by Marlow to his fiancée, compounding his guilt. Having misled her, Marlow instantly begins a monologue to himself, his own admission of the suppressed reality. As Kurtz's confidant and mute accessory, it is clear that Marlow is as much of a sinner as Kurtz, as the final chapter exemplifies.

Nathaniel Hawthorne, was particularly intrigued by guilt, sin, their associated concepts and outcomes, composing various novels and stories relating to such issues, that Renu Josan investigates in her chapter. Hawthorne's narratives of fiction comprise of complementary moral, social and psychological dynamics. The individual sense of a general, overarching collection of ethical values that must govern moral action, as enshrined in a particular cultural, religious or philosophical understanding, is not apparent in Hawthorne's works. Instead, intricate relations and moral quandaries are linked together by Hawthorne to navigate the unguided depths of personal moral action. With its focus on secret desire and its ramifications, *The Scarlet Letter* is underpinned by a discussion of public and private moral principles, the characteristics of moral virtue and general moral issues. Our modern views on the forbidden romance of Dim- mesdale and Hester are likely to be removed from Hawthorne's own, however his audience was New England of the 1800s, reflecting the Puritan tendencies in his own upbringing. Nevertheless, although moral principles are explored in Puri- tan context, it is individual emotions and integrity that are focused on rather than religious institutions' own sanctions. Therefore, the means through which public and private expectations of morality can be brought to equilibrium, moral discernment and moral parameters are the primary focus of Josan's discussion.

The appeal of sin is emphasised as a notion in Eloïse Sureau-Hale's essay. She posits that there is extreme temptation from having something one cannot have, or a proscribed relationship or illicit activity. Treading the line of what is wrong and what is permissible is incredibly attractive; individuals who forgo the constraints of law and morality to act and transgress as they please are a pleasure to explore through novels. Of all the literary works emerging from France in the 1800s, debauchery is analysed in an unparalleled way in *Maldoror* released in

1869 by the Count of Lautréamont, the pseudonym of Isidore Ducasse. This work comprises of moral contraventions and sin, rather than being a discussion of such activity. Sureau-Hale's chapter is concerned with three varied aspects of transgression and sin, namely sin in relation to the audience, to the narrative and the novel. The continued sinning and incentivising of other characters to sin engaged in by Maldoror, the work's protagonist, is explained and reasons posited. The reduction of human beings to the lower rings of natural order, while insect life is revered, is assessed for its intent. With humans typically being situated as the pinnacle of God's creation, is this an intentional reduction of their prominence? Furthermore, with the writer's manner becoming increasingly depraved, we can observe the manifestation of sin on further sin, thus translation is investigated as a kind of wrongdoing. For the depravity of the text to be authentically engaged with, the methods of obliging the audience to engage are assessed. Thus, through consuming the text in a prurient manner, the audience is compelled to commit sin, flitting between sadistic gratification and guilt. Sureau-Hale's chapter ends with an assessment and conception of the entire novel's intention, drawing on the moral principles of the 1800s to assess Ducasse's debauched mind and depravity. Academics are still analysing *Maldoror* in the new millennium: the novel is still widely read, as explained alongside the situating of the novel in a thoroughly modern context.

Lastly, *The Nemesis of Faith* (1849), written by James Anthony Froude, is assessed by Paola Partenza. This text is rarely investigated in the contemporary period, while its provocative queries made it foremost among the challenging texts of the period. Ciaran Brady stresses that republication of the novel occurred at numerous points, regardless of its burning at Exeter College refectory at one point. Indeed, Froude himself exclaimed in 1880 to John Skelton, a friend, that he would not permit its reprinting while he was alive. Julia Markus noted that *The Nemesis of Faith* was perceived as a handbook for adultery and a representation of Froude's personal psyche, while Froude declared the text to be a "dust storm". Opposition was open to Froude and his text among the severest conservatives of the period, with easy disagreement on the basis of the text's perceived immoral nature. Given the emphasis on appropriate behaviour in Victorian society, the *Nemesis of Faith* was condemned for its unprincipled character. However, Partenza suggests that Froude was seeking to show that the liberty of humans is the straightforward reason for sin, with individuals unable to elude the intricate net of uncertainties that results and that characterises sin; in this regard, the text may be considered as a precise assessment of the theological and moral spheres.

Paola Partenza

Igor Djordjevic

"The breath of kings" and "the pleasure of dying": Political "Sin" and Theatrical Redemption in *Eikon Basilike*

During the English Reformation the Providential approach to interpretations of the present and the past, combined with the notion of the Divine Right of Kingship, expanded the notion of "sin" to the political realm. Protestant polemics such as William Tyndale's *Obedience of a Christian Man* (1528), John Ponet's *Shorte Treatise of Politike Power* (1556), and John Knox's *First Blast of the Trumpet against the Monstruous Regiment of Women* (1558) demanded religious righteousness from English monarchs in return for obedience, while the Elizabethan Homilies thundered injunctions against the potential "sins" of the *subject* against the sovereign: regicide, rebellion, treason, and sedition. Under Elizabeth, an "unofficial" popular discourse couched in historical and cultural memory emerged and dwelled on the English *kings'* "sins" of misrule against their subjects in chronicles, conduct-books, and various *de casibus* tragedies of the *Mirror for Magistrates* and the professional stage.[1] The ruler's cardinal "sin" in each disastrous case proved to be his violation of what James I termed the "reciprock" duties of the monarch and subject to each other, whereby the king's selfless labour in the interest of the commonweal earns the subject's "good opinion" and "love".[2] While various chronicles and Mirrors countered vicious rulers with exemplars of politic virtue, when England's history leapt onto the professional stage, audiences beheld spectacles of royal misgovernment: the preferment of sycophantic favourites, faction at court, and abuses of royal prerogatives.[3] Shakespeare's *Henry VI* plays resurrect the Wars of the Roses and follow the "contention" for the crown, while virtually all the characters on stage in one way or another subvert the period's political ideals.[4] Shakespeare's plays

---

1 See P. Budra, A Mirror for Magistrates *and the* De Casibus *Tradition*, Toronto, University of Toronto Press, 2000.

2 James I, *The True Law of Free Monarchies and Basilikon Doron*, ed. by D. Fischlin and M. Fortier, Toronto, Centre for Reformation and Renaissance Studies, 1996, pp. 51–52, 62.

3 See I. Djordjevic, *Holinshed's Nation: Ideals, Memory, and Practical Policy in the* Chronicles, Burlington, Ashgate, 2010.

4 The "trilogy" was composed out of sequence, and most probably in collaboration: *The First*

about Henry VI, whose long reign was the greatest national disaster staged for English theatrical audiences, paradoxically also provide the formula for his redemption in national memory. It proves to be a recipe potent enough not only to sublimate the Wars of the Roses in Tudor culture's formative memory, but, apparently, also to change the minds of many who witnessed Charles I executed as "a Tyrant, Traitor, Murderer and Public Enemy to the Good People of this Nation"[5] in their *present*.

Within a few days of the execution a book attributed to Charles throughout the seventeenth century emerged from the presses, the *Eikon Basilike*,[6] whose most famous reader John Milton excoriated it precisely for its dramatic flair.[7] Much has been said already about the *Eikon*'s inception, generic and rhetorical structure, popularity and reception, and Charles's Christic "self-fashioning" that enraged his enemies.[8] What has not been explored sufficiently, however, is how a particular type of *dramatic self-fashioning* contributed to its remarkable success.

This essay will explore how conventional dramatic tropes in the *Eikon* cast Charles as a tragic hero, imitating the fall of Henry VI, another "sinner" against

---

Part of the Contention of the Two Famous Houses of York and Lancaster (1590–1591) renamed in the First Folio as *2 Henry VI*, *The True Tragedy of Richard Duke of York and the Good King Henry the Sixth* (1591) renamed *3 Henry VI*, and *1 Henry VI* (1592); the dating and all citations of Shakespeare's plays refer to *The Oxford Shakespeare: The Complete Works*, ed. by S. Wells, G. Taylor, et al., Oxford, Clarendon Press, 2005.

5 The text of the verdict, reprinted in *Eikon Basilike with Selections from Eikonoklastes by John Milton*, ed. by J. Daems and H. F. Nelson, Peterborough, ON, 2006, p. 319.

6 The "Anglesey Memorandum" published as a preface to Milton's 1690 edition of *Eikonoklastes* revealed the authorial contribution of John Gauden, future Bishop of Exeter; the current consensus is that the *Eikon* was a collaborative text (E. Skerpan Wheeler, Eikon Basilike *and the Rhetoric of Self-Presentation*, in *The Royal Image: Representations of Charles I*, ed. by T. N. Corns, Cambridge, Cambridge University Press, 1999, pp. 135–136; N. McDowell, *Milton, the* Eikon Basilike, *and Pamela's Prayer: Re-Visiting the Evidence*, in "Milton Quarterly", XLVIII, 2014, pp. 225–226).

7 P. Stevens, *Milton, Drama, and the Nation*, in *The Elizabethan Theatre XV*, ed. by C. E. McGee and A. L. Magnusson, Toronto, Meany, 2002, pp. 320–321; S. Achinstein, *Milton and King Charles*, in *The Royal Image: Representations of Charles I*, ed. by T. N. Corns, Cambridge, Cambridge University Press, 1999, p. 154. Also see R. Helgerson, *Milton Reads the King's Book: Print, Performance, and the Making of a Bourgeois Idol*, in "Criticism", XXIX, 1987, pp. 1–25.

8 S. Greenblatt, *Renaissance Self-Fashioning: From More to Shakespeare*, Chicago, University of Chicago Press, 1980; E. P. Skerpan, *Rhetorical Genres and the* Eikon Basilike, in "Explorations in Renaissance Culture", XI, 1985, pp. 99–111; E. Skerpan Wheeler, Eikon Basilike *and the Rhetoric of Self-Representation*, cit.; R. Wilcher, *What Was the King's Book for?: the Evolution of* Eikon Basilike, in "The Yearbook of English Studies", XXI, 1991, 218–228; L. B. McKnight, *Crucifixion or Apocalypse?: Refiguring the* Eikon Basilike, in *Religion, Literature, and Politics in Post-Reformation England, 1540–1688*, ed. by D. B. Hamilton and R. Strier, Cambridge, Cambridge University Press, 1996, pp. 138–160; A. Lacey, *The Cult of King Charles the Martyr*, Woodbridge, UK, Boydell Press, 2003, pp. 14–15, 29–31; K. Sharpe, *Image Wars: Promoting Kings and Commonwealths in England, 1603–1660*, New Haven, Yale University Press, 2010, pp. 391–403.

the commonwealth who suffered rebellion, deposition, and possibly regicide, but whose reputation had been considerably rehabilitated.[9] Shakespeare's theatrical tropes in his memorial re-enactment of the traumatic birth of English national and political selfhood effectively pardoned a royal misfit. The *Eikon* borrows some of these dramatic devices to re-imagine and redeem Charles who in his textual afterlife also became, in Andrew Marvell's terms, a "royal actor" on the "tragic scaffold" of the nation's memory.[10] David Cressy has argued that "the battle to control the meaning and memory of the English revolution began even as its earliest episodes were unfolding."[11] I will show how by the 1640s Shakespeare's histories infused with the "rhetoric of commonweal" became "inherited and remembered images" that the *Eikon* employed "to refute the charge that Charles Stuart was a 'Man of Blood'" and to redeem the memory of a king who waged war against his own people.[12]

"Keep me from the strife of tongues"

If the Regicides were in fact aware of the power of emblems, symbols, tableaus, and timing in drama – whether professional or amateur, in a theatre or on a civic pageant's scaffold – their decisions reveal a dangerous underestimation of the early modern stage. Not only was the king's execution "staged" on 30 January, 1649, a day for which the Book of Common Prayer appointed the reading of Matthew's Gospel account of the Crucifixion,[13] but Charles was also allowed to deliver an unscripted oration to an audience of thousands (something a far more stage-aware Elizabeth did not allow her troublesome cousin Mary) in which he memorably cast himself as a pious "Martyr of the people", a loving sovereign

---

9 See *The Mirror for Magistrates*, ed. by L. B. Campbell, Cambridge, Cambridge University Press, 1938, pp. 211–219; S. Daniel, *The Civil Wars Between the Houses of Lancaster and York*, ed. by L. Michel, New Haven, Yale University Press, 1958; G. F. Biondi, *An History of the Civil Wars of England between the Two Houses of Lancaster and York,* trans. by H. Carey Earl of Monmouth, London, 1641. For the uses of history as critique in Charles's reign, see K. Sharpe, *Image Wars*, cit., pp. 271–274, 326–327; I. Djordjevic, *Holinshed's Nation*, cit., pp. 178–196, 244–246.

10 A. Marvell, "An Horatian Ode upon Cromwell's Return from Ireland", in *The Poems of Andrew Marvell*, ed. by Nigel Smith, Harlow, UK, Pearson Education Limited, 2007, ll. 53–66.

11 D. Cressy, *Remembrancers of the Revolution: Histories and Historiographies of the 1640s*, in "Huntington Library Quarterly", LXVIII, 2005, p. 258.

12 K. Sharpe, *Image Wars*, cit., pp. 183–184; K. Sharpe, *The Royal Image: An Afterword*, in *The Royal Image: Representations of Charles I*, ed. by T. N. Corns, Cambridge, Cambridge University Press, 1999, p. 291; E. Skerpan Wheeler, Eikon Basilike *and the Rhetoric of Self-Representation*, cit., p. 127.

13 L. B. McKnight, *Crucifixion or Apocalypse?*, cit., p. 138.

victimized by his unruly subjects, and to exchange his "corruptible" for an "incorruptible Crown".[14]

Marvell's "Horatian Ode upon Cromwell's Return from Ireland", composed between June and July 1650,[15] is a memorial act, recalling this event in England's immediate past. Marvell famously depicts king Charles I's "memorable hour" on the scaffold before the Banqueting House in theatrical terms: Charles was a "royal actor" who "adorned" the "tragic scaffold", a "memorable scene" where he "nothing common did, or mean" and finally "bowed his comely head / Down as upon a bed" while "round the armed bands / Did clap their bloody hands".[16] Although Charles's tragic dignity depends on the reader's appreciation of the inauthentic connotations of the language of performance,[17] we should remember that theatricality and an attention to performative self-presentation (despite past assumptions based on his speech-impediment) were important components of Charles's kingship, and helped establish the cult of King Charles the Martyr almost immediately after his execution.[18] Marvell's scene, therefore, can be read as a literary account of the king's last self-conscious performance in the "sacrificial drama Cromwell and the army [...] scripted for him",[19] but also as a reflection of an older dramatic tradition of kingly dying which the *King's Book* had already appropriated.

Eikon Basilike emerged within days of the execution, but William Dugard's elaborate edition printed on 15 March, which Milton called the "best", effectively converted the work "from a personal narrative to an 'experience'".[20] It contains accretions that combine a personal account of recent history with religious meditations in the vein of John Donne's *Devotions Upon Emergent Occasions* (1624),[21] alternating between dramatic soliloquy and prayer, and concludes with

---

14 Charles's speech is reprinted in *Eikon Basilike*, ed. by J. Daems and H. F. Nelson, cit., pp. 319–324. Interestingly, Milton saw Charles's performance in the *Eikon* as an imitation of his grandmother Mary rather than of Christ (*Eikonoklastes*, London, 1649, p. 238).

15 N. Smith, *The Poems of Andrew Marvell*, cit., p. 267.

16 A. Marvell, "An Horatian Ode upon Cromwell's Return from Ireland", cit., ll. 53–66. For Marvell's poem in the context of other "regicide elegies" see A. Garganigo, *Mourning the Headless Body Politic: the Regicide Elegies and Marvell's "Horatian Ode"*, in "Exemplaria", XV, 2003, pp. 509–550.

17 T. Bower, *Sacred Violence in Marvell's Horatian Ode*, in "Renascence: Essays on Values in Literature", LII, 1999, p. 83.

18 See K. Sharpe, *Image Wars*, cit., pp. 137–403; A. Lacey, *The Cult of King Charles the Martyr*, cit., pp. 4–17.

19 T. Bower, *Sacred Violence in Marvell's Horatian Ode*, cit., p. 84.

20 E. Skerpan Wheeler, *Eikon Basilike and the Rhetoric of Self-Presentation*, cit., p. 132. By the end of 1649, thirty-five English editions were published, whereas the total count of separate printings rises to sixty-nine if we consider "foreign translations, abridgements, selections, versifications, and musical settings" (R. Helgerson, *Milton Reads the King's Book*, cit., p. 8).

21 A. Lacey, *The Cult of King Charles the Martyr*, cit., p. 9.

two accounts of his parting with his children, as well as other paratextual additions.[22] Unenthusiastic about the "work assign'd rather, then by [him] chosen", Milton questions Charles's authorship and gripes about the futility of rebutting the "soliloquies" of a dead king, thereby repudiating the possibility of persuading his audience; but the *Eikon's* reliance on dramatic devices that had become a part of English culture by 1649 was always going to make it propagandistically powerful.[23]

The reader experiences the first-person narrative as a soliloquy and the "moment" of the character's speech is taken to be the eternal *now*, the *nunc stans* of print. The sections of the text were composed at different times between 1642–1649, but because they are undated and in no chronological order, the readers respond to the royal voice as the audience in a theatre would: his disjointed memorial account of the events explains the causes of his fate, while his prayers, curses, and prophesies, the typical rhetorical modes of a stage tragic hero, locate him in prison, facing death. Following dramatic convention, any early modern reader would have felt compelled to believe a deathbed oration, and the *Eikon's* veracity comes from its funereal ethos as a parting soliloquy. It inducts the reader into a privileged audience of those close enough not only to hear the king's voice, but sometimes even his thoughts whispered to himself.

Not all soliloquys are the same, however. Conventionally, it is a stream of consciousness audible only to the theatrical audience. But sometimes, as in the case of Richard III with whose "deep dissembling" Milton compared Charles,[24] it can be calculated, indicating the character's desperate need to win audience sympathy. Charles's soliloquy, Milton suggests, is not "innocent" and whatever revelations are made are not "unmediated"; this kind of "I" is "perjured", but its "illusion of transparency [...] makes it a resource of enormous persuasive

---

22 A. Lacey, *The Cult of King Charles the Martyr*, cit., p. 86.

23 J. Milton, *Eikonoklastes*, cit., sig. B1ʳ-B2ᵛ, C1ʳ. The Council of State, considering the *Eikon* politically and polemically subversive, tasked Milton with composing a response which was published in October 1649; "By the time Milton completed his official refutation, a popular cult of Charles the martyr was already established and any hope of an immediate popular base for the new regime undermined" (K. Sharpe, *Image Wars*, cit., p. 403). For Milton's rhetorical approach to his task, see D. Shore, *"Fit though Few": Eikonoklastes and the Rhetoric of Audience*, in "Milton Studies", XLV, 2006, pp. 129–148; J. Egan, *Oratory and Animadversion: Rhetorical Signatures in Milton's Pamphlets of 1649*, in "Rhetorica", XXVII, 2009, pp. 189–217; and S. Achinstein, *Milton and King Charles*, cit., pp. 141–161. For Milton's understanding of "theatricality" in the *Eikon*, see R. Helgerson, *Milton Reads the King's Book*, cit.; P. Stevens, *Milton, Drama, and the Nation*, cit.; and *Milton's Janus-Faced Nationalism: Soliloquy, Subject, and the Modern Nation State*, in "Journal of English and Germanic Philology", C, 2001, 247–268; and T. P. Anderson, *Performing Early Modern Trauma from Shakespeare to Milton*, Burlington, Ashgate, 2006, pp. 178–180.

24 J. Milton, *Eikonoklastes*, cit., p. 11.

power".[25] In Charles's musings Milton heard tonal and intentional echoes of Shakespeare's Richard III, but the *Eikon* reveals Charles's hermeneutic subtlety in differentiating the effects of his "private" musings.

In Shakespearean drama sometimes the speaker unwittingly reveals too much to others in the stage-world, like the unsuspecting Juliet to the concealed Romeo who "stumble[d] on her counsel"[26] at the start of the balcony scene. Charles, like Juliet, is indignant at an unauthorized eavesdropping: his letters, captured at Naseby in 1645, were "taken and divulged", revealing his attempts to secure foreign and Irish aid against Parliament. At the start of his long self-defense, Charles exclaims, "I wish My Subjects had yet a clearer sight into My most retired thoughts" and says he was motivated by "love and care [...] not more to preserve My own Rights, than to procure their peace and happiness, and that extreme grief to see them both deceived and destroyed".[27] But he never explains his secretive dealings against his own people. Eventually, perhaps realizing that his actions were indeed indefensible, Charles employs a weighty trope, kingship's patriarchal analogue, the cornerstone of Stuart royalist discourse which will "sustain" his cult after 1649,[28] and chastises those who divulged his correspondence for "forgetting that duty of modest concealment, which they owed to the Father of their Country, in case they had discovered any real uncomeliness; which I thank God they did not; who can, and I believe hath made Me more respected in the hearts of many".[29] Charles's argument suggests this was not only a crime of overhearing hidden political thoughts in an unauthorized soliloquy;[30] it was one deserving a biblical curse. Notwithstanding his bizarre equivocating denial that "spins" a positive result from the unwelcome revelations, his initial analogue reveals quite clearly that his shame at having his mind known by his subjects was an emotional torment that could only be likened to Noah's embarrassment and anger after discovering his son had gawked at his drunk father's exposed genitals.[31] Charles passes dramatically from a Juliet-like embarrassment to a Hamlet-like railing against an imagined negative public image,[32] but because he never refutes the "facts" revealed by his secret correspondence, his rhetorical squirming reveals the humanity of the king. If he shows more of it, his readers may even be willing to forgive him for his treachery.

---

25 P. Stevens, *Milton, Drama, and the Nation*, cit., p. 308.

26 *Romeo and Juliet*, II.i.94–95.

27 *Eikon Basilike*, cit., p. 160.

28 See Sir Robert Filmer, *Patriarcha*, London, 1680; A. Lacey, *The Cult of King Charles the Martyr*, cit., p. 6.

29 *Eikon Basilike*, cit., p. 162.

30 Somewhat similar to the rage of the Democrats following the email "hacks" of the 2016 American election.

31 Genesis 9, 21–27.

32 *Hamlet*, II.ii.552–582.

And that is precisely what the *Eikon* does. Charles sets the record straight and inscribes his memory in the minds of his rebellious subjects even though they had cut off his head. The *Eikon* repeatedly acknowledges the king's politically imprudent missteps, which could prove as devastating to his political reputation as the surviving historiographic record of other kings who suffered rebellions, such as John, Edward II, Richard II, and Henry VI. But Charles is able to "appeal to a common subjectivity or identity"[33] and to inscribe his own memory by articulating his motivations instead of outsourcing it all to unreliable historiographers who, in his view, would propose "misconstructions of [his] actions, (which are prone to find more credulity in men to what is false, and evil, than love or charity to what is true and good)".[34] Thus he sets the stage for his redemption: not as a *king* but as a *man*.

"Loyal injuries" and "good intentions"

At the first sign of danger to his throne, Shakespeare's Richard II exclaims:

Not all the water in the rough rude sea
Can wash the balm from an anointed king.
The breath of worldly men cannot depose
The deputy elected by the Lord.[35]

The sacrosanct political dictum of the Divine Right of Kingship also contains the magical formula that can undo it. The "breath of worldly men" cannot depose God's own anointed monarch, but what about the breath of the king himself? "How long a time lies in one little word!" Bolingbroke muses after Richard reduced his banishment, implying that a royal utterance has the power even to abolish time, "such is the breath of kings".[36] By the end of *Richard II* it becomes clear that the power of royal utterance alone can undo the Divine unction of a king, as Richard not only "unkings" himself in the deposition scene, but also remolds his "sinful" identity into something he can neither identify in a looking glass, nor comprehend in the abstract, nor ultimately accept in the final imprisoned hours of his life.[37]

---

33 P. Stevens, *Milton, Drama, and the Nation*, cit., p. 321.
34 *Eikon Basilike*, cit., p. 105. Charles's implicit complaint about the unreliability of historiography was common among historians of the first half of the seventeenth century; see I. Djordjevic, *Holinshed's Nation*, cit., pp. 207–236, and *"No chronicle records his fellow": Reading Perkin Warbeck in the Early Seventeenth Century*, in "Renaissance and Reformation", XL. 2, 2017, pp. 63–102.
35 *Richard II*, III.ii.50–53.
36 *Richard II*, I.iii.206–208.
37 *Richard II*, IV.i.263–292 and V.v. 1–66.

Charles famously questioned and defied the "lawful authority" of the court and the judges that tried and sentenced him, and ultimately upstaged his enemies in the spectacle and "multi-media event" of his execution.[38] His literary persona in the *Eikon* is as great a devotee to the concept of Divine Right as Shakespeare's Richard, and almost perfectly echoes Richard's delight when he imagines himself a veritable *roi-soleil* and "this thief, this traitor" Bolingbroke's terror at seeing him "rising in [his] throne, the east" and proving unable "to endure the sight of day / But self-affrighted, trembl[ing] at his sin".[39] Charles is an annoyed Sun-King when he muses upon his enemies' seizure of "the King's Magazines, Forts, Navy, and Militia" at the start of his troubles in 1641–1642, and suggests that his self-restraint should not be seen as an abdication of Divine Right:

> Although I can be content to Eclipse My own beams, to satisfy their fears; who think they must needs be scorched or blinded, if I should shine in the full lustre of Kingly Power, wherewith God and the Laws have invested Me; yet I will never consent to put out the Sun of Sovereignty to all Posterity, and succeeding Kings …[40]

The difference between Richard and Charles is in their self-fashioning *after* the decline of their respective political fortunes. Richard typically rants and threatens cosmic destruction only to collapse into tearful tirades of impotent self-pity. Charles, on the other hand, exaggerates his benevolence and mercy, and redefines himself as a righteous sufferer, "for never were any Princes more glorious, than those whom God hath suffered to be tried in the furnace of afflictions, by their injurious Subjects".[41] He frequently reminds his reader of his royal forbearance because he is one of those "honoured with the name of *Gods*" and that "none may without sin seek to blot them out".[42]

The *Eikon*'s emphasis on Charles's patient suffering inevitably separates him from the histrionic Richard II, but it brings him close to another Shakespearean king. Henry VI, in the eyes of his greatest enemy Richard of York, is "Not fit to govern and rule multitudes" because his head "doth not become a crown" while his "hand is made to grasp a palmer's staff, / And not to grace an aweful princely scepter".[43] This dyslogistic view of the king is not disputed by anyone in the stage world; not by his wife nor the loyal Lancastrians. His character in the trilogy, like in the chronicles, is an exemplum of indecorous traits for an English king: infantility, effeminate weakness, uxoriousness, and bookish aloofness from the proper duties of governance. But he is also an exemplar of holiness. For audi-

---

38 K. Sharpe, *Image Wars*, cit., pp. 381–390.
39 *Richard II*, III.ii.43–49.
40 *Eikon Basilike*, cit. p. 90.
41 Ivi, p. 128.
42 Ivi, pp. 128–129.
43 *2 Henry VI*, V.i.94–98.

ences watching the plays sequentially, as a grand narrative of the Wars of the Roses, there is no doubt that Henry's political folly and impotence gradually erode his royal authority, but his piety never comes in question.

Noticing Charles's pious self-fashioning, Milton attacks the *Eikon* as an inauthentic "Stage-work", but then bizarrely echoes a common slur used against Henry VI in Shakespeare's plays: "To pray and not to govern is For a Monk and not a King".[44] Charles confesses a number of political "sins", but he insists his actions were inspired by an "upright intention, to Thy glory, and My People's good".[45] Although such rhetorical formulas, yoking piety with chivalric service to the commonweal, are conventional in English "commonwealth discourse",[46] Charles's presentation of the entire political imbroglio in spiritual terms, whereby Parliament plays God's instrument to bring him and people "unfeignedly to repent for [their] sins",[47] effectively denies Parliament's representative authority. Consequently, in the *Eikon*, the "history" of the political and military catastrophe of Charles's reign is emplotted as a spiritual journey of personal enlightenment and salvation, and it recasts his struggles to defend his people and his legal rights as love's war.[48]

Like Shakespeare's Henry VI who attains his greatest wisdom atop his molehill, in the thick of the internecine bloodbath,[49] Charles is "the Man of Sorrows"[50] who has a moment of dazzling clarity when he is able to understand the cause of his rebellious subjects' motivations:

> I had the Charity to interpret, that most part of my Subjects fought against My supposed Errors, not My Person; and intended to mend Me, not to end Me: And I hope that God pardoning their Errors, hath so far accepted and answered their good intentions, that as he hath yet preserved Me, so he hath by these afflictions prepared Me, both to do him better service, and My people more good, than hitherto I have done.
> I do not more willingly forgive their seductions, which occasioned their loyal injuries, than I am ambitious by all Princely merits to redeem them from their unjust suspicions, and reward them for their good intentions.[51]

His words present an exegetical loop as he interprets his subjects' motivations which were, previously, shaped by their misapprehension of his own person and motives. In an echo of Brutus's subtle differentiation of the variable readings of

---

44 J. Milton, *Eikonoklastes*, cit., pp. 172, 174.
45 *Eikon Basilike*, cit., p. 53.
46 See I. Djordjevic, *Holinshed's Nation*, cit.
47 *Eikon Basilike*, cit., p. 53.
48 Ivi, pp. 67, 152.
49 *3 Henry VI*, II.v.
50 A. Lacey, *The Cult of King Charles the Martyr*, cit., p. 107.
51 *Eikon Basilike*, cit., p. 122.

the effects of conspiratorial knives on Caesar's dead body,[52] Charles appreciates his subjects' "loyal injuries" and prays that their "good intentions" be rewarded rather than their hurtful actions. Consequently, as he approaches his death he becomes more explicit in asking his people to judge him not by his warlike actions against them, but by his hitherto hidden *loving* motives.

Charles's literary persona throughout seems metahistorically aware of the public impact of the eventual printing of these purportedly *private* "papers" composed in "his solitudes and sufferings".[53] His last prayer, "Hear my prayer, O Lord, which goeth not out of feigned lips",[54] is not only decorous for a religious suppliant, but a crucial metanarrative definition of textual authority. The narrator's impending death defines his ethos and provides an exegetical instruction to the reader to treat the entire *Eikon* as a deathbed confession. Allowed to eavesdrop on Charles's advice to his eldest son to be "confident (as I am) that the most of all sides, who have done amiss, have done so, not out of malice, but misinformation, or mis-apprehension of things",[55] the readers witness the king excuse his subjects' flawed hermeneutics as the root cause of the conflict. Might they not be expected, in turn, to believe in his good intentions and pardon his "sinful" actions just as he had theirs? What could be more reminiscent of a dramatic scene than this *anagnorisis*?

"Speak me fair in death"

Charles I "made marriage and paternity the dominant themes of his representation and the language of love a discourse of rule".[56] The *Eikon*'s tragic encodation of Charles as a "loving husband and tender father whose affective familial relationships symbolized his loving union with his people"[57] employs stock affective tropes from Renaissance drama that "humanize" characters whose high political status or their historical and cultural remoteness keep them apart from the common experience of the average theatre-goer. For example, Marlowe's Edward II, an imprudent king who elevated the unworthy and antagonized his nobles, humanizes himself as the caring father of a "little boye".[58] Talbot, the terror of the French and the flower of English chivalric heroism, dies

---

52 *Julius Caesar*, II.i.172–174.
53 *Eikon Basilike*, cit., p. 138.
54 Ivi, p. 178.
55 Ivi, p. 191.
56 K. Sharpe, *Image Wars*, cit., p. 140.
57 Ivi, p. 396.
58 *Edward II*, IV.iii.48 (*The Complete Works of Christopher Marlowe*, vol. II, ed. by F. Bowers, Cambridge, Cambridge University Press, 1981).

in the last battle of the Hundred Years War not as a victim of treacherous French arms but as a grieving father, almost a prototype for Lear's last scene, with his "poor boy" in his arms.[59] John Ford's *Perkin Warbeck*, using the same affective tropes, makes tragic and comprehensible even the death scene of possibly the greatest historical enigma: the mysterious Perkin himself, who exits the world a "King o'er death", a loving husband torn away from his loving wife.[60]

The *Eikon*, possibly also borrowing from contemporary "loyalist poetry", sounds the same affective notes to emphasize the "physical and emotional suffering of the martyr [...] to enlist the sympathy of the audience".[61] He is a husband who misses his wife, a responsible and caring king who addresses a miniature *Fürstenspiegel* in the penultimate chapter to the future Charles II, but also a loving parent who parts from his son on a human level, asking that he be remembered as a "Father that loves You".[62] Charles imitates the conventional history-play hero's stage death: he has a prophetic vision of the "severer scatterings which will certainly befall such as wantonly refuse to be gathered to their duty", and concludes with "Farewell, till We meet, if not on Earth, yet in Heaven".[63]

The tragic effect of a hero's death in a history play is both a product and a conduit of memory, and history plays frequently stage moments of metahistorical awareness. Shakespeare's Henry V and his "band of brothers" at Agincourt, and Brutus and Cassius after killing Caesar, all envision posterity's memory of them. Caroline histories do the same: Ford's Lord Stanley inscribes Clifford's foul memory at his fall in *Perkin Warbeck*, while Robert Davenport stages Fitzwater's tender care for King John's chronicle reputation in *King John and Matilda*.[64]

But metahistory is not only a specialty of the history genre. Famous tragic heroes express metahistorical awareness and a similar desire to control memory: Hamlet commands Horatio to remain alive and "draw [his] breath in pain / To tell [his] story", while Othello, right before he ends his guilty life, asks the witnesses, "in your letters, / When you shall these unlucky deeds relate, / Speak of me as I

---

59 *1 Henry VI*, IV.vii.23–32.
60 *Perkin Warbeck*, V.iii.207. All citations of Ford's play refer to J. Ford, *The Chronicle History of Perkin Warbeck: A Strange Truth*, ed. by P. Ure, London, Methuen, 1968.
61 K. Sharpe, *Image Wars*, cit., p. 307; A. Lacey, *The Cult of King Charles the Martyr*, cit., p. 13.
62 *Eikon Basilike*, cit., pp. 74–75 and 183–195.
63 Ivi, p. 181.
64 *Henry V*, IV.iii.40–67; *Julius Caesar*, III.i.112–119; *Perkin Warbeck*, II.ii.90–91; R. Davenport, *King John and Matilda*, sig. I2^v (London, 1655); also see I. Djordjevic, *King John (Mis)Remembered: The Dunmow Chronicle the Lord Admiral's Men, and the Formation of Cultural Memory*, Burlington, Ashgate, 2015, p. 152 and 163–164, and *"No chronicle records his fellow"*, cit., p. 101.

am. Nothing extenuate, / Nor set down aught in malice".[65] Even the comedic character Antonio, believing himself in the last act of his tragedy while readying his breast for Shylock's knife, attempts to control the history of his life and its interpretation when he instructs Bassanio: "Say how I lov'd you. Speak me fair in death, / And, when the tale is told, bid [Portia] be judge / Whether Bassanio had not once a love".[66] Hamlet, Othello, and Antonio exert control over memorial narratives because the stage world at their departure is still unsettled and capable of misreading the tumultuous events they caused. Aware at the moment of his parting with his son that "history" is not over and its outcome unknown, Charles attempts to exert the same hermeneutic control over memory.[67]

Charles's most poignant "humanizing" scene is his parting with his daughter Elizabeth and his youngest son Henry, both of whom were Parliament's captives. Two renditions of the scene are appended to the *Eikon*: an anonymous third-person account and one "from the Lady Elisabeth's own Hand".[68] The effect of the two texts lies in the amplification of the young children's vulnerability, as Charles warns them that they (and their two brothers) will be beheaded should they be caught or if they disobey their evil captors. The loving father gives a message for their mother, "That His thoughts had never strayed from Her, and that His Love should be the same to the last", and then asks Elizabeth "not to grieve for Him, for He should die a *Martyr*".[69] A year later Elizabeth herself would die in captivity, adding the aura of a victim of Parliamentary tyranny to the composite authorial ethos of an "innocent babe" and obedient daughter serving her father's memory. This posthumous "authority" that precludes the bias of a politically-motivated supporter[70] shapes the exegesis of her paratextual additions to the *Eikon*. After 1650 a reader of Elizabeth's passages, notwithstanding the possibility of its being a "pathetic appeal staged by the *Eikon*'s compiler",[71] might well have read the *Eikon* not only as a true account of the king's suffering and death, but also as a *family* tragedy – a common sentiment among the survivors of two civil wars.[72]

Charles's farewells, final meditations, and prayers at Carisbrooke Castle further evoke parallels with famous royal prisoners in castle dungeons audiences had seen and heard soliloquize for two generations: Marlowe's Edward II at

---

65 *Hamlet*, V.ii.300–301; *Othello*, V.ii.349–352.
66 *Merchant of Venice*, IV.i.272–274.
67 *Eikon Basilike*, cit., p. 188.
68 Ivi, pp. 212–214.
69 Ivi, p. 213.
70 N. Jacobs, *Robbing His Captive Shepherdess: Princess Elizabeth, John Milton, and the Memory of Charles I in the* Eikon Basilike *and* Eikonoklastes, in "Criticism", LIV, 2012, p. 228.
71 Ivi, p. 232.
72 E. Skerpan Wheeler, Eikon Basilike *and the Rhetoric of Self-Representation*, cit., p. 133.

Berkley, Shakespeare's Richard II at Pomfret, and Henry VI in the Tower. Charles's decision to "die a martyr", reported by his daughter, makes *Eikon Basilike* his "'Limbo Rhetoricke,' the prison in which he meditates his pillory", and converts the civil wars "into a psychomachia".[73]

Imitatio Christi

One of the most striking rhetorical features of the *Eikon* is Charles's performance as a Christ-like martyr. He compares his political struggles with Parliament in 1641 to Christ's three temptations, recasts his "retirement from Westminster" following his failed attempt to arrest five members of Parliament in 1642 as suffering for "conscience" and a choice of the "crown of thorns", and thereafter continues to posture more and more overtly as a Christic sacrificial king.[74] Frequently quoting Christ's words to express his suffering and his faith in the forgiveness of his "sins and the sins of [his] people", he even prays, "forgive them! O my Father, for they know not what they do".[75]

　　The Christological parallels intensify as Charles narrates his political fall as a "passion". Anticipating defeat, he recasts "the many Jealousies raised and Scandals cast upon the King, to stir up the People against Him" as "false aspersions".[76] His Judas is played by the Scots, and his only regret is that his ransom's "price should be so much above my Saviour's".[77] Thereafter, Charles embraces "captivity or death" as "the price of [his subjects'] redemption", and "happily" accepts rather to "suffer for [his subjects] than with them" to "redeem [him]self".[78] After offering his penitential forgiveness to all who have wronged him,[79] in his last *original* prayer he declares that he will not "forget to imitate My crucified Redeemer, to plead their ignorance for their pardon; and in My dying extremities to pray to thee O Father to forgive them, for they know not what they did".[80]

73　E. P. Skerpan, *Rhetorical Genres and the* Eikon Basilike, cit., p. 103.

74　*Eikon Basilike*, cit., pp. 68, 72, 86.

75　Ivi, pp. 87–88.

76　Ivi, pp. 121, 123.

77　Ivi, p. 166.

78　Ivi, p. 167.

79　Ivi, p. 177.

80　Ivi, p. 183. Milton's discovery of the plagiarized "Pamela" prayer lifted from Sir Philip Sidney's *Arcadia* has unsettled readings of the "sincerity" of Charles's prayers; for a concise overview of the debate, see N. McDowell, *Milton, the* Eikon Basilike, *and Pamela's Prayer: Re-Visiting the Evidence*, cit. This prayer comes before the supplementary materials added in Dugard's text, and in my view, reflects Charles's "original" ethos. Lana Cable argues that Milton read the *Eikon*, and the Pamela prayer in it, as an "idolatry of words. Words exploited

By absorbing Renaissance martyrological and Christological rhetorical conventions the *Eikon* rehabilitated Charles's reputation and effectively turned the propagandistic tide against Parliament,[81] but this achievement was not entirely unprecedented. Henry VI, who lost France and presided over the implosion of his domestic realm, experienced a similar historiographic and cultural redemption after his death. The early modern cultural view of that miserable ruler is in large measure reflected in Shakespeare's similarly Christological transformation of Henry from a bad king to a sacrificial lamb.

Shakespeare's Henry VI's association with Christ begins in the parabolic scene of the false miracle at St. Albans in which he is a foil to Humphrey of Gloucester.[82] Whereas Henry's actions and words in the scene connote equally well a pure innocent or a naïve simpleton, by invoking Christ's words "blessèd are the peacemakers on earth" and putting them into practice[83] he shows the audience glimpses of his transcendent aura. His mind in the clouds with God's angels, Henry fails the test of worldly prudence and proves himself antithetical to the Renaissance princely ideal,[84] leaving the contemporary audience "aghast at such single-minded piety which has rendered the king politically blind and lame",[85] but the same moment also invests him with uncommon sanctity.

Like Shakespeare's Henry VI, Charles remembers the beginning of the "insolency of the Tumults" and is perplexed by his selfish enemies' "unlawful and irreligious means" whose "force must crowd in what Reason will not lead".[86] Further echoing Henry who made "frowns, words, and threats" his only "war",[87] Charles recalls Uxbridge, where he never "did [...] think it a diminution of Me to prevent them with Expresses of My desires, and even importunities to Treat: It being an office, not only of humanity, rather to use Reason, than Force; but also of Christianity to *seek peace and ensue it*".[88] "[W]illing to condescend, as far as

---

for purposes alien to their original intent, words devitalized and dispirited by rote recitation, words distanced from the tensive impulses of thought and feeling that generated them [...]" (*Milton's Iconoclastic Truth*, in *Politics, Poetics, and Hermeneutics in Milton's Prose*, ed. by D. Loewenstein and J. G. Turner, Cambridge, Cambridge University Press, 1990, p. 146). Nicole Jacobs suggests that Milton's comments can be read as "part of his strategy to critique the use of the privileged words of a king's daughter without explicitly insulting the thirteen-year-old girl who was being held captive by Parliament" (*Robbing His Captive Shepherdess*, cit., p. 242).

81 A. Lacey, *The Cult of King Charles the Martyr*, cit., pp. 51–53.
82 *2 Henry VI*, II.i.
83 *2 Henry VI*, II.i.34, 58–61.
84 For example, see Sir Thomas Elyot, *The Boke Named the Governour*, London, 1531; Sir Geoffrey Fenton, *A Forme of Christian Pollicie*, London, 1574.
85 R. Knowles, *Shakespeare's Arguments with History*, New York, Palgrave, 2002, p. 29.
86 *Eikon Basilike*, cit., p. 61.
87 *3 Henry VI*, I.i.72–73.
88 *Eikon Basilike*, cit., p. 147.

Reason, Honour, and Conscience would give [him] leave",[89] Charles, like Henry, fashions himself a reluctant warrior, and conceals his political imprudence in the negotiations behind a pious regard for his "conscience".

Henry's sacrificial kingship is born in the moment when his uncle, the "Good Duke" Humphrey of Gloucester who stood as the last bulwark of political stability, falls to the ring of conspirators in a scene replete with Christic sacrificiality.[90] In his last moments, Gloucester fancies himself a "shepherd" beaten from the king's side as the "gnarling" wolves close in,[91] and his words introduce a crucial sacerdotal metaphor of kingship. To be a "good shepherd" is to follow in the footsteps of Christ; but Christ is also the "Lamb of the Lord" in His sacrificial function. Gloucester's words initially cast Henry in the role of the vulnerable sheep, but as Henry inherits royal power from the fallen Lord Protector, he also becomes the kingdom's new princely "shepherd".[92]

Ironically, when the war breaks out, Henry has time to sit on a molehill and ponder the cataclysm, wishing he led the life of a "homely swain", a shepherd.[93] Conventional pastoral tropes of princely escapism in the context of a history play unsettle the wishes of a failed shepherd of a kingdom devoured by baronial wolves and suggest he would be no better at herding actual sheep; but the scene is not intended to be comedic. As he becomes a moral commentator of the tableau of internecine strife Henry, whom war had deprived of the metaphoric role of the shepherd of the kingdom, begins to speak and act as a composite Christic *shepherd-sacrificial lamb* figure. Having never ordered, witnessed, nor been accused of any Lancastrian atrocities, he attains an aloofness from the worldly chaos of his kingdom. His musings on the national tragedy of fathers and sons pressed into infanticide and parricide by the murderous gentry elevate him morally above the butchery of the civil war, and they reinforce his "holiness" and pity for all men. In this new ethos Henry at last understands *realpolitik* of which

---

89 Ibidem.

90 *2 Henry VI*, III.i.165–169. Shakespeare's Christic construction of Humphrey's character echoes the topoi used in the "tragedies" of Eleanor Cobham and Duke Humphrey in *The Mirror for Magistrates*, where Cardinal Beaufort as chief plotter and judge is called "Cayphas" (*The Mirror for Magistrates*, cit., Tragedy 28, l. 114), while the Duke compares the plotters against him to "Herode and Pylate" who come "to iudge Iesu Christ" (*The Mirror for Magistrates*, cit., Tragedy 29, l. 371).

91 *2 Henry VI*, III.i.189–194.

92 This was a commonplace of Renaissance political discourse. Fenton defines the decorous duties of a governor in figurative terms: "Togither with this order of iustice, the gentilman is bound to keepe and defend his tenants, as the shepherd his Lambes, that they be not deuoured of vagabounds, spoyled of theeues, and mordered by robbers: But as the good shepherd watcheth ouer his flocke, defends it from woulues [...]" (*A Forme of Christian Pollicie*, cit., sig. Qq3ᵛ). The analogues were still commonplace in sermons of Charles's time (K. Sharpe, *Image Wars*, cit., p. 188).

93 *3 Henry VI*, II.v.1–54.

he had shown himself to be absolutely incapable in the past, and predicts the political machinations of both Margaret and the "subtle orator" Warwick in their courtships of Lewis of France.[94] At his capture, he laments the fickleness and stupidity of man, adapting Christ's line: "Ah, simple men, you know not what you swear".[95] The difference between his use of the Christic line here and at St. Albans is that he now exhibits an understanding of dissembling human nature in a way that only Gloucester could do. This "transcendent" Henry combines the spirituality of a saint with the understanding of a prudent man.[96]

Imitating Henry – whose tearful, swooning *pietà* over Gloucester's corpse dissociated him from the bloodthirsty court factions[97] – Charles laments a noble subject whom he could not save. Charles's Gloucester, of course, is Strafford who, in the eyes of many, was convicted in a sham trial.[98] Grieving, Charles waffles between excusing his apparent powerlessness with the biblical "Maxim, *Better one man perish (though unjustly) than the people be displeased or destroyed*"[99] and confessing his "sin of betrayal" in the prayer: "forgive me that act of sinful compliance […] [s]ince I had not the least temptation of envy, or malice against him, and by my place should, at least so far, have been a preserver of him, as to have denied my consent to his destruction".[100] Occasionally Charles may blame his advisors for "miscarriages in Government", but on the whole he insists that all his acts of political imprudence must be read as pacific acts of Christian virtue, attested by his "Prayers and Tears".[101]

"Sad stories of the death of kings"

Whether a hero's death is deemed *tragic* – in the *de casibus*, Senecan, or Aristotelian sense – depends on his last moment. Renaissance playwrights offer diverse death-scenes, each a coded message about the world or life itself. In history plays, as in the chronicles that conclude reigns with a summative *laus*, the death scene frequently defines one's cultural memory and reputation. Shakespeare's plays show that he understood the impact of a death scene. His historical source for *Richard II*, the 1587 edition of Holinshed's *Chronicles*, provides three versions of the king's death. Shakespeare chooses the most "heroic" one, the fight

---

94 *3 Henry VI*, III.i.28–54.
95 *3 Henry VI*, III.i.82.
96 Compare *3 Henry VI*, III.i.99–100 and *2 Henry VI*, III.i.189–194.
97 *2 Henry VI*, III.i.198–222; III.ii.39–55, 136–148.
98 K. Sharpe, *Image Wars*, cit., p. 379.
99 *Eikon Basilike*, cit., p. 55; John, 18, 14.
100 Ivi, p. 56; A. Lacey, *The Cult of King Charles the Martyr*, cit., pp. 26–27.
101 Ivi, pp. 81, 88, 103.

against eight assassins (four of whom Richard dispatches before he is killed from behind) rather than the long and undramatic death from "forced famine" or Richard's equally anticlimactic "voluntarie pining of himselfe".[102] These kinds of authorial choices define the character of a king in a work but they also shape cultural memory, much like Richard II's cynical view of kingship as a "hollow crown" is based on his understanding of history as a catalogue of kingly deaths.[103] In the case of Henry VI, whose death exists in two chronicle versions, Shakespeare chooses Sir Thomas More's unattributed rumour, again most likely for purely dramatic reasons.[104] But the "justice" of a king's "cause" is strongest for those who maintain it if the king is sent off with a "bang."[105]

As England experiences its first outbreak of violence in the Cade Rebellion, Henry echoes Christ's dying words, suggesting an allegorical merger of the land and the king's body: "O, graceless men; they know not what they do".[106] England torn by civil war indeed becomes, as the Bishop of Carlisle prophesies in Shakespeare's *prequel*, "the field of Golgotha and dead men's skulls",[107] where Henry suffers a passion and tragic death. In his last scene Henry resurrects his prophetic role from the molehill. Echoing Gloucester's death scene, Henry revives the pastoral metaphors, casting his departing jailer in the role of wayward shepherd and embraces the role of the lamb abandoned to the wolf or butcher.[108] Having already divested himself of a princely shepherd's duties when he laid his hands on the head of Richmond as "England's hope",[109] Henry becomes the sacrificial lamb in his passion's last station.

Henry employs his oracular powers as a weapon against his demonic adversary, envisioning Richard's short-lived, bitter victory in a defiant invective, but he is silenced mid-sentence, as part of Richard's recently discovered hatred of "words."[110] Henry's vituperative tone is not incongruous with his past ethos of a meek champion of holiness; having demonized Richard from the outset,[111] in his final hour he is a holy warrior defying the incarnation of Satan. His death is a

---

102 R. Holinshed, *The Chronicles of England, Scotland and Ireland,* vol. III, London, 1587, pp. 516–517.

103 *Richard II,* III.ii.151–166. For a detailed study of the formation of early modern cultural memory of a king, see I. Djordjevic, *King John (Mis)Remembered,* cit.

104 R. Holinshed, *Chronicles,* cit., p. 690; I. Djordjevic, *Holinshed's Nation,* cit., p. 218.

105 Shakespeare's John exits with something of a "whimper" (I. Djordjevic, *King John (Mis)Remembered,* cit., pp. 40–41).

106 *2 Henry VI,* IV.iv.37.

107 *Richard II,* IV.i.135.

108 *3 Henry VI,* V.vi.7–9.

109 *3 Henry VI,* IV.vii.68.

110 *3 Henry VI,* V.v.43.

111 *3 Henry VI,* V.vi.4.

"defeat"[112] only if we ignore the Christic dimension of his character, shut our ears to his prophecy, and do not recognize the eventual "resurrection" of his "line" in the future Henry VII. The unfolding of history and the audience's memory make Henry's death a Christological victory and redemption.

Crowns – paper and incorruptible

In early modern historical drama, the mode of dying inscribes a life's meaning. Put differently, a culture's artistic representation of a historical character's death can reflect posterity's sublimation of historical trauma into a political message. Any character's Christlike sacrificiality may attempt to redeem him in an audience's imagination, but the effect is not automatic. Shakespeare's rendition of Henry VI's story, true to its chronicle source, also offers an example that problematizes the use of the sacrificial trope.

Richard of York, historically and in Shakespeare's rendition, is very far from Christ's example – both spiritually and politically. York brings a mixed bag of dynastic "right", Machiavellian political savvy, bravery, English patriotic Gallophobia, seditious skullduggery, fierce family loyalty, vengefulness, and an unforgettable death scene. Shakespeare's York's death comes from a confluence of several memorial threads from fifteenth- and sixteenth-century chronicle accounts,[113] repackaged as a new cultural memory birthed on the professional stage. York endures a mock-crucifixion wearing a paper crown, responds to the jeers of his executioners, and dies in a moment of righteous, defiant self-sacrifice, certain of his soul's heavenly destination.[114] Although the mock-coronation as a piece of political theatre staged by Margaret is obviously aimed at demeaning York as a false "king", a pretender destroyed by his vaulting ambition, the scene's echoes of famous Protestant martyrdoms turn the audience against Margaret's theatrical motives:

> the deep tradition of Christ's abjection immediately allows an inversion in which the intended symbol of degradation is converted to a marker of spiritual glory. In this vein, martyrs themselves often adopt one or another form of "crowning" in direct emulation

---

112 A. Leggatt, *Shakespeare's Political Drama: The History Plays and the Roman Plays*, New York, Routledge, 1988, p. 243.

113 See P. Strohm, *York's Paper Crown: "Bare Life and Shakespeare's First Tragedy"*, in "Journal of Medieval and Early Modern Studies", XXXVI, 2006, pp. 75–101. The Christological charge of the episode, combining the paper crown and the explicit comparison of his tormentors to the Jews, comes from Whethamsted; Abraham Fleming adds it into the 1587 text of Holinshed's *Chronicles*, whence it is adopted by Shakespeare (P. Strohm, *York's Paper Crown*, cit., pp. 83–84, 86–87; I. Djordjevic, *Holinshed's Nation*, cit., pp. 193–196).

114 *3 Henry VI*, I.iv.168–169, 178–179.

of Christ. [...] Whether manipulated by resourceful victims or introduced by sympathetic viewers or commentators, the elements of mock-crowning can hardly resist assimilation to the ubiquitous and more powerful imagery surrounding the sacrifice of Christ. [...] Once this kind of imagery begins to flow, York's tormentors have already in effect lost their representational game.[115]

In both chronicle and play York attains a level of "Christliness" thanks to the iconographic echoes of Calvary, but we should remember that there was never any cultic adoration of his remains and no historical attempt to canonize him – even for political purposes in the way Henry VII sought to capitalize on Henry VI's cult. Comparing York's to Henry's association with Christic tropes, it is debatable to what extent Shakespeare's York can be considered "redeemed". How ready is the audience to forget or forgive York's many political "sins" against his country, such as his complicity in the death of Gloucester, or his seditious use of Cade? York's tragic ethos in the scene is reliant on his affective self-fashioning as a grieving father of a butchered boy, a male hero mocked and tortured by the despicable French monster-queen, and the audience – insofar as it is responding to the political *Trauerspiel* before their eyes[116] – is less keen to see York as Christ than it is to see the sadistic roles of the Gospels' mocking soldiers or Whethamsted's "Jewes"[117] played by Margaret and her Lancastrian henchmen. The audience inevitably recognizes the Christic tropes in York's death scene, but Shakespeare's figurative encodation of the tableau redirects its dominant emotional response, anger, from the victim to the executioners.

Charles's literary death in the *Eikon* combines the most effective dramatic elements of the deaths of Henry VI and York, including the exegetical redirection of the Christological tableau. Imitating the arc of Henry's stage tragedy, Charles defines his enemies as false shepherds (or wolves in sheep's clothing), prays for the attributes of a decorous shepherd of his realm, and finally becomes the meek sacrificial lamb who will "have the pleasure of dying, without any pleasure of desired vengeance"; he is a sacrificial king whose "death be the wages of [his] sin" amid the hope that his "sins" will be "so remitted, that they shall be no ingredients to imbitter the cup of my death" while pardoning the sins of those "who are most guilty of [his] destruction".[118] Charles imagines his impending execution as a theatrical tableau in which he will play the part of Christ: "My

---

115 P. Strohm, *York's Paper Crown*, cit., pp. 83–84.
116 Ivi, pp. 94–97.
117 Matthew, 27, 27–31; Mark, 15, 16–20; John, 19, 2–3; quoted in P. Strohm, *York's Paper Crown*, cit., p. 87.
118 *Eikon Basilike*, cit., pp. 90, 101, 199, 202. McKnight notes that Charles uses the shepherd-image sparingly "probably because by this time anti-episcopal tracts had so thoroughly turned this metaphor against the king's original allies, the bishops [...]" (*Crucifixion of Apocalypse?*, cit., p. 145).

Friends and loving Subjects" will be "helpless Spectators" while "My Enemies" will be "insolent Revilers and Triumphers over Me, living, dying, and dead [...] My Enemies (being more solemnly cruel) will, it may be, seek to add (as those did, who Crucified Christ) the mockery of Justice, to the cruelty of Malice".[119] Like York, Charles intends to use the Christic encodation of the tableau as a means to hijack the show and reinscribe its political message, from "the public dispatch of a traitor" to "the creation of an English martyr".[120] History has confirmed the *Eikon's* remarkable success in converting Charles's "martyrdom" into the ultimate propagandistic weapon while stopping just short of advocating an idolatrous cult of sainted kingship.[121]

"Remember"

Moments before he laid his head on the block, king Charles removed his cloak with his "George" and handed it to William Juxon, Bishop of London, saying, "Remember".[122] In the years that followed, that word became a rallying cry for the king's scattered followers, and an inscription on the king's memorial bust in the chapel of Charles's prison at Carisbrooke Castle. Perhaps most interestingly, it inspired an anonymous *de casibus* "news-drama" published months after the execution: *The Famous Tragedie of King Charles I.*[123] Though Charles appears in the title and is mentioned frequently, he does not appear at all until the epilogue when, like Gloucester's body in *2 Henry VI*, his corpse is "revealed" to the audience by the Chorus beside the bodies of the lords Capel, Hamilton, and Holland, executed in March for Charles's cause. The memory of his "murther'd" body is inscribed with meaning, even if the Chorus can do no more than offer wishful thinking about history's end in a moment when England will "see these Monsters fall and rot, / By God and virtuous men forgot."[124] A king who had co-opted the language of dramatic art to snatch a propagandistic victory from the jaws of political and military defeat, now becomes the stuff of drama itself, a prop in a stage tableau that simultaneously reflects and re-inscribes his cultural

---

119 Ivi, p. 197.
120 K. Sharpe, *Image Wars*, cit., p. 390.
121 See E. P. Skerpan, *Rhetorical Genres and the* Eikon Basilike, cit., pp. 104–106.
122 The jewel in the insignia of the Order of the Garter; for the text of Charles's speech on the scaffold, see *Eikon Basilike*, cit., pp. 319–324.
123 The play, possibly written by Samuel Sheppard, may have been printed before May, 1649 (B. Ravelhofer, *News Drama: the Tragic Subject of Charles I*, in *English Historical Drama, 1500–1600*, ed. by T. Grant and B. Ravelhofer, New York, Palgrave Macmillan, 2008, pp. 179–180, 192).
124 *The Famous Tragedie of King Charles I*, London, 1649, pp. 42–43; B. Ravelhofer, *News Drama: the Tragic Subject of Charles I*, cit. p. 186.

memory. If Milton's *Eikonoklastes* "fought over the interpretation of history" with *Eikon Basilike* and sought to "demystify" it,[125] Charles's almost immediate reincarnation in a tableau of Civil War historical "crypto-drama" was a premonition of Milton's inevitable failure.[126]

As we have seen, early modern drama was able to redeem the political "sins" of medieval misfit kings and to re-exemplify them in English cultural memory. Although the *Eikon* is primarily the *history* of a king who suffers an insurrection, defeat, and execution, it finds emulative exemplars for its hero not in the Tudor chronicles or in Stuart politic historiography but in their dramatic avatars, the stock-figures of martyred kingship on the Renaissance stage.[127] Shamelessly adopting the various affective tropes from drama, it lays particular emphasis on the most potent set of Christological *topoi* of sacrificial kingship.

York's historical "mock-coronation" and "mock-crucifixion" adopts "elements of the sacred" and proves how "dangerous" it is for any ruler to try to "consolidate their authority by denying their subjects the dignity of sacrifice".[128] The orchestrators of the historical fifteenth-century "theater of cruelty" and their Shakespearean avatars "gifted" York with a potent "sacrificial death";[129] but the Regicidal Court did the same for Charles in 1649. The "labile and shifting" popular reconceptualization of the *images* of these two kings confirms the people's exegetical authority over history, or, indeed that "people make kings".[130]

125 S. Achinstein, *Milton and King Charles*, cit., pp. 153–154.

126 T. Grant and B. Ravelhofer, *Introduction* to *English Historical Drama, 1500–1660*, ed. by T. Grant and B. Ravelhofer, cit., p. 21.

127 R. Zaller, *Breaking the Vessels: The Desacralization of Monarchy in Early Modern England*, in "The Sixteenth Century Journal", XXIX, 1998, pp. 757–778, p. 769.

128 P. Strohm, *York's Paper Crown*, cit., p. 88.

129 Ivi, pp. 76, 88.

130 I. Djordjevic, *Holinshed's Nation*, cit., pp. 171–172; K. Sharpe, *The Royal Image*, cit., p. 303; E. Skerpan Wheeler, *Eikon Basilike and the Rhetoric of Self-Representation*, cit., p. 137.

Margarete Rubik

Scoffing at Sin: Aphra Behn, Restoration Culture and the Concepts of Sin and Guilt

Restoration free-thinking

Restoration culture was in many ways a reaction against the religious zeal and Puritan austerity of the Commonwealth era. In a violent swing of the pendulum, the dominant baroque court culture after 1660 was rationalist and sceptical in thinking and licentious in morals, often with a lascivious excess which gratuitously set out to scandalize orthodox religious believers. The newly restored monarch, Charles II, made his many mistresses conspicuous in public; many of the aristocrats and court wits were, if not unbelievers, at least free-thinkers who in their lives and works poked fun at religious beliefs and bourgeois moral norms. The age saw what devout Christians regarded as an unprecedented assault on things formerly held sacred.[1] A spirit of mockery and scoffing informed many literary works of the period, though few authors outed themselves as downright atheists,[2] but continued to call themselves Christians, albeit doubting the superstitions and moral oppressiveness of Church teachings. There was good reason for such caution: blasphemy was still a common-law offence, which was punishable by a fine, imprisonment, corporeal punishment or even death. A charge of blasphemy could be used as a legal instrument to persecute atheists, though such a charge was generally difficult to prove. Besides, the terms blasphemy and free-thinking were often loosely applied to any kind of heresy, immorality and scandalous behaviour.[3]

Not even Thomas Hobbes, whose philosophy had a considerable influence on

---

1 Cf. J. Spurr, *The manner of English Blasphemy, 1676-2008*, in *Religion, Identity and Conflict in Britain: From the Restoration to the Twentieth Century, Essays in Honour of Keith Robbins*, ed. by S. J. Brown, F. Knight and J. Morgan-Guy, London/New York, Routledge 2016 [2013], pp. 27–45, p. 31.

2 Cf. Ivi, p. 29.

3 P. Zagorin, *Cudworth and Hobbes on Is and Ought*, in *Philosophy, Science and Religion in England 1640-1700*, ed. by R. Kroll, R. Ashcraft, P. Zagorin, Cambridge, Cambridge University Press 1992, pp. 128–148.

the thinking of the social elite, called himself an atheist, though his concepts of God were certainly heterodox and had nothing to do with the personalized God of Christian belief. For the purpose of investigating the culture's attitude to sin, several of Hobbes' theories are of particular interest. Hobbes argued for a moral relativism: in his view, good and evil are mere preferences,[4] depending on what is likely to further our newest appetite. Nothing is intrinsically good or bad, unless it is defined as such by the law,[5]– i. e., a sin is what the monarch chooses to call sin:[6] moral obligation thus comes from the Sovereign, not God. The passions in themselves are no sin, but natural to man's nature. And the belief in rewards and punishments after death, according to Hobbes, destabilizes the state.

Such precepts were, of course, quite antagonistic to the Christian "legacy of guilt, shame and moral self-examination", the belief in an immortal soul and the faith in eternal blessing or damnation in the afterlife.[7] Moreover, it is essential to remember that Restoration libertines such as Rochester reinterpreted Hobbes, or gave him what critics call a "partial reading",[8] combining his philosophy with Epicureanism and the teachings of Lucretius,[9] who was a genuine atheist. For Hobbes, the original state of nature he had envisaged involves humankind in a condition of anarchy, in which every man is a wolf to every other man (*homo homini lupus*) and the life of human beings is "nasty, brutish, and short";[10] only by ceding freedom to a sovereign in a social contract can this state of a war of all against all be ended. The Restoration libertines, however, extolled this state of nature, in which the individual is free to indulge his appetites and enter into a riotous pursuit of pleasure.

In order to express their derision of piety and traditional ethical norms, the wits of the time in their works portrayed rakish characters who flaunt heterodox morals and scoff at religion and virtue. Scoffing, at the time, was defined by Henry Hooton as

> [...] prophanely making Holy Writ the subject of their Mirth, and Drollery, ridiculing Vertue and Religion [...] laughing all Piety out of Countenance. [...] to speak loosely, and wantonly, about holy Things, or Persons [...] or to turn the Sentences and Phrases of the Holy Scripture into Jest, and Ridicule [...].[11]

---

4 W. Chernaik, *Sexual Freedom in Restoration Literature*, Cambridge, Cambridge University Press, 1995, p. 32.

5 P. Zagorin, cit., p. 131.

6 W. Chernaik, cit., p. 30.

7 Ivi, p. 27.

8 G. Southcombe, and G. Tapsell, *Restoration Politics, Religion, and Culture. Britain and Ireland 1660–1714*, London, Palmgrave Macmillan, 2010, p. 157.

9 Cf. W. Chernaik, cit., p. 22.

10 T. Hobbes, *Leviathan* [1651], ch. XII, http://www.gutenberg.org/files/3207/3207-h/3207-h. htm#link2HCH0013.

11 H. Hooton, *A Bridle for the Tongue* (1709), qtd. in Spurr, cit., p. 29.

Aphra Behn's religious scepticism

Aphra Behn was the first professional English dramatist who lived by her pen, writing a remarkable number of plays, narratives and poems. She was a staunch supporter of the Stuart kings and in her works propagated Tory standpoints. She was friends with several court wits, knew and admired the Earl of Rochester, and shared the sceptical thinking of her contemporaries. Nonetheless, the word 'sin' occurs surprisingly often in her oeuvre, but it is largely divorced from an ethical context and frequently used with an explicit intention of banter and irreverence. 'Sin' as Behn uses the term denotes predominantly fornication – whores follow a 'trade of sin'; but behind such an appellation there is no sense of peccability or guilt. Female chastity is merely regarded as a cultural norm, and a regrettable one to boot. People, she argues, were happier in a fabled semi-paradisiacal earlier age when women were free to follow their sexual desires like men, without becoming social outcasts when they lose their virginity outside of marriage. In her poem entitled "The Golden Age", she complains that "the Gods / By teaching us Religion first, first set the World at Odds"[12] and penalized the innocent enjoyment of sexuality. She returns to the attack on contemporaneous commandments of sexual purity and prudish behavioural norms in *The Emperor of the Moon*, when she calls "Custom, that dull excuse for fools, / Who think all virtue to consist of rules."[13] Similarly, in her famous narrative *Oroonoko*, she describes the primordial South American Caribs as representing to her

> an absolute *Idea* of the first State of Innocence, before Man knew how to sin: And 'tis most evident and plain, that simple Nature is the most harmless, inoffensive and vertuous Mistress. 'Tis she alone, if she were permitted, that better instructs the World, than all the Inventions of Man: Religion wou'd here but destroy that Tranquillity, they possess by Ignorance; and Laws wou'd but teach 'em to know, Offence, of which now they have no Notion.[14]

Like many of her contemporaries, she was distrustful of the belief in miracles and supernatural events and regarded Lucretius as a liberator from the religious tyranny[15] exercised by a clergy trying to inculcate fear of divine punishment into the believers. In a poem to the translator Thomas Creech she expressed her admiration of the Roman philosopher, whose materialist philosophy, she claims,

---

12 A. Behn, *The Golden Age* in *The Works of Aphra Behn*, ed. by J. Todd, Vol. 1, London, Pickering, 1992, pp. 30–35, p. 31. All subsequent references to Behn's works are to Todd's edition.

13 A. Behn, *The Emperor of the Moon*, in *The Works of Aphra Behn*, ed. by J. Todd, Vol. 7, London, Pickering, 1996, pp. 153–207, I. 1, p. 161.

14 A. Behn, *Oroonoko*, in *The Works of Aphra Behn*, ed. by J. Todd, Vol. 3, London: Pickering, 1995, pp. 51–119, p. 59.

15 Cf. Chernaik, cit., p. 22.

[...] Pierces, Conquers and Compels,
As strong as Faiths resistless Oracles.
Faith the Religious Souls content,
Faith the secure Retreat of Routed Argument.[16]

She was also one of the first writers, in her "Essay on Translated Prose" (prefaced to her translation of Fontenelle's *Discovery of New Worlds*), to employ bible criticism, collating the Scriptures with historical documents and showing that many biblical stories cannot be taken literally, although (out of caution or genuine conviction) she did not put into question divine revelation as such. A certain hostility towards Scripture, however, is typical of the free-thinkers of the age,[17] and in her translation of Fontanelle's *History of Oracles and the Cheats of the Pagan Priests* Behn implicitly also attacks the practices of the Christian clergy.[18]

Several characters in Behn's works display the same religious scepticism and rationalist attitude as their author. In *Oroonoko*, the eponymous hero, tutored by an exiled French atheist, rejects the doctrine of the Trinity; yet he is far more admirable and honest than the treacherous Christian slave traders and white colonists. Gayman in *The Luckey Chance* is not "such a coxcomb to believe" that the devil himself has summoned him to a rendez-vous:

Spirits, ghosts, hobgoblins, furies, fiends and devils
I've often heard old wives fright fools and children with,
Which, once arrived at common sense, they laugh at.
No, I am for things possible and natural:
Some female devil, old, and damned to ugliness,
And past all hopes of courtship and address,
Full of another devil called desire,
Has seen this Face---this---Shape---this Youth
And thinks it worth her Hire.[19]

Another character in the play is a similar unbeliever: "The devil, sha! There is no such animal in nature."[20] It was sentiments like these that infuriated clergymen like Joseph Glanvill, rector of Bath Abbey:

---

16 A. Behn, *To The Unknown Daphnis on his Excellent Translation of Lucretius*, in *Works*, Vol. 1, cit., pp. 25–28, p. 26.

17 I. Rivers, *Reason, Grace, and Sentiment. A Study of the Language of Religion and Ethics in England, 1660–1780. Vol. 2: Shaftesbury to Hume*, Cambridge, Cambridge University Press 2000, p. 8.

18 Cf. J. Todd, *The Secret Life of Aphra Behn*, London, Andre Deutsch, 1996, p. 399.

19 A. Behn, *The Luckey Chance*, in *Works*, Vol.7, cit., pp. 209–284, II. 1, p. 238.

20 Ivi, IV. 1, p. 262.

Heaven and Hell are become words of sport, and Devils and Angels, Fairyes and Chimeras: Tis Foppish to speak of Religion, but in Railery; or to mention such a thing as Scripture; except to be burlesque and deride it.[21]

Methods of scoffing at sin in Behn's works

Besides a voicing of scepticism, how was scoffing at sin concretely accomplished in Restoration writings? Spurr[22] enumerates a number of strategies writers employed to give a good dose of offense to the pious, without opening themselves up to full-fledged charges of blasphemy. These include unserious allusions and irreverent mockery, pseudo-arguments and the reduction ad absurdum of religious opinions; a dismissive attitude towards virtue; the assumption of outrageous ethical positions; irony and equivocation; all delivered in a tone of wit and raillery to challenge laughter and make the audience complicit in the joke.

On a quite simple level, Behn uses religious words mockingly and un-seriously in an erotic context. Her most famous play, *The Rover*, is especially rich in such 'blasphemous' uses: Hellena, who against her will is destined to become a nun, would rather find a handsome lover: "[…] no, I'le have a *Saint* of my own to pray to shortly, if I like any that dares venture on me."[23] In order to get her into bed quickly, the eponymous protagonist asserts that "long fasting Child, spoils a Man's Appetite"[24] and that he "hate[s] long Graces – come let's retire and fall to".[25] When he has money, he invites his friend to "sacrifice"[26] to the bottle. When he encounters an unknown woman in a garden, he takes her for a god-sent call to sexual activity – "what has God sent us here! – a Female!"[27] – and tries to rape her. Although, according to the legal understanding of the time, the charge of rape did not apply if a prostitute was involved, the woman in question, in fact, is not a whore. As many critics have pointed out, the scene quite dramatically shows the nasty and violent side of the rake-hero. A similarly facetious use of religious vocabulary is involved in calling a pretty whore "the greatest blessing this wicked World can afford us"[28] in *The Feign'd Curtizans*; and one of the eponymous heroines, in turn, asserts tongue-in-cheek, that courtesan is "a Noble title and

---

21 J. Glanvill, *Seasonable Reflections* (1676), qtd. in Spurr, cit., p. 31.

22 Ivi, p. 32.

23 A. Behn, *The Rover*, in *The Works of Aphra Behn*, ed. by J. Todd, Vol. 5, London, Pickering, 1996, pp. 445–521, I. 1, p. 458.

24 Ivi, III. 1, p. 479.

25 Ivi, V. 1, p. 516.

26 Ivi, III. 1, p. 478.

27 Ivi, III. 5, p. 486.

28 A. Behn, *The Feign'd Curtizans*, in *The Works of Aphra Behn*, ed. by J. Todd, Vol. 6, London, Pickering 1996, pp. 83–159, I. 1, p. 92.

has more *Votaries than Religion* [...].”[29] In *The City Heiress*, another lewd rake looks forward to an assignation at Church “with the dearest she-Saint, and I hope sinner.”[30] Church is conceived of as a place of seduction; the term ‘saint’ has lost all religious meaning and simply refers to the hypocrisy of the ecclesiastical meeting-place, where he hopes to conjoin with anyone but a saintly woman.

Occasionally, what is and what is not a sin is not so easy to determine. Daughters were expected to obey their fathers, but the spectators undoubtedly sympathized with the heroines of *The Rover* or *The Feign’d Curtizans*, who feel they have a right to rebel against being forced to marry a man they abhor or being confined in a nunnery against their will. A forced marriage, one such victim asserts, is mere “Prostitution in the lewdest manner, without the Satisfaction”;[31] indeed, “such a Wedlock would be worse than Adultery with another Man.”[32]

Not even adultery is always a clear-cut case. Previous engagements were considered legally binding in the Restoration period, and could be enforced by legal action if vows had been exchanged before witnesses: another marriage would in such cases have been regarded as bigamous, hence establishing a (semi-)moral right of the first lover to claim the woman. The problem is, however, that few of these fictional vows were made before witnesses (which is why ‘Heaven’ is occasionally invoked as a witness). Besides, few of Behn’s married female protagonists (as opposed to the girls who run away to escape such a fate) were actually forced into a marriage – rather, they married rich old men for financial security. Now that they regret their choice, they try to find excuses to please themselves – though the audience is hardly encouraged to take such a cynical view of their doings, but in comedies generally sides with the young lovers. In *The False Count*, Julia has ethical scruples to cuckold her nasty old husband – “Aye, but the Sin [...]!” – but is assured by her casuistic maid that “Heav’n wou’d forgive it, for this match of yours, with old *Francisco*, was never made there”; and since Julia had made her first vows to her lover, this, she is persuaded, would make “lying with old *Francisco* ... flat Adultery”.[33] Her lover Carlos is more pragmatic: he reasons that “Adultery is a less sin than Murther”[34] and therefore, in the guise of the Turkish sultan, frightens her husband into yielding up his wife to him. Absurdly, when he learns the truth, Francesco is particularly angry because, for him, Julia’s adultery with Carlos may have involved the same sin, but less honour as if she had slept with a monarch.[35]

---

29 Ivi, II. 1, p. 103.
30 A. Behn, *The City Heiress*, in *Works*, Vol. 7, cit., pp. 1–77, I. 1, p. 14.
31 A. Behn, *The Younger Brother*, in *Works*, Vol. 7, cit., pp. 355–417, I. 1, p. 368.
32 A. Behn, *The Rover*, in *Works*, Vol. 5, cit., I. 1, p. 457.
33 A. Behn, *The False Count*, in *Works*, Vol. 6, cit., pp. 299–356, I. 2, p. 308.
34 Ivi, II. 2, p. 320.
35 Ivi, V. 1, p. 353.

Occasionally, some such definitions of what is, and what is not, a sin are quite hair-raising and idiosyncratic, ridiculing traditional ethical standards and Christian teaching. Thus the jealous Galliard, who hopes to sleep with one of the (feigned) courtesans, has the presumption to argue that whoredom is acceptable for a woman, but "bartering words with fools"[36] – i. e., prospective rivals – is unforgivable. Willmore preposterously contends that the courtesan Angellica's sin lies in her high price (i. e., in the cardinal sin of pride in her beauty), and not in her unchastity, and that she should therefore give herself to him for free. Equally outrageous is his sophistry that if Florinda, the innocent woman he happened upon in the garden, sleeps with him,

> [...] there will be no sin in't, because 'twas neither designed nor premeditated. [...] indeed, should I make Love to you, and vow you fidelity- - -and swear and lye till you believ'd and yielded- - -that were to make it wilful fornication- - -the crying sin of the nation- - -thou art, therefore (as thou art a good Christian) oblig'd in Conscience to deny me nothing.[37]

Not only does he argue that impromptu intercourse is no sin (as if it did not involve the wilful consent of both parties), he tops his sophism by claiming that it would be Christian charity for her to comply. A related proposition is advanced by the hypocritical preacher Tickletext, who reasons that *"the sin of wenching lay in the habit only"*, so that he is "free to recreate himself" with a whore once.[38]

Young cavaliers regard the cuckolding of middle class citizens as a war against their Puritan and Whig opponents and as a sign of the superior potency of their Royalist ideology. Thus the two Royalists in *The Roundheads* wage war against the leaders of the Commonwealth by seducing their wives, regarding it as legitimate to "live on the sins of the Spoiler".[39]

Behn herself was somewhat idiosyncratic in her sense of what constitutes a mortal sin. She showed remarkable understanding and sympathy for female characters who transgress the rules of sexual continence; sexual relations between lovers, in her eyes, can only be a venial offence – if any. In a poem paraphrasing the Lord's Prayer, she muses on the verse "And forgive us our Trepasses" in the following way:

> How prone we are to Sin, how sweet were made
> The pleasures, our resistless hearts invade!
> Of all my Crimes, the breach of all thy Laws
> Love, soft bewitching Love! has been the cause;

36　A. Behn, *The Feign'd Curtizans*, in *Works*, Vol. 6, cit., IV. 2, p. 136.
37　A. Behn, *The Rover*, in *Works*, Vol. 5, cit., III. 5, pp. 486–487.
38　A. Behn, *The Feign'd Curtizans*, in *Works*, Vol. 6, cit., III. 1, pp. 121–122.
39　A. Behn, *The Roundheads*, in *Works*, Vol. 6, cit., pp. 357–424, II. 1, p. 379.

Of all the Paths that Vanity has trod,
That sure will soonest be forgiven of God [...].[40]

That she was not alone in this attitude, is ironically evinced in the Epilogue to her posthumously performed play *The Widdow Ranter*, which praises the author – a famed writer of erotic verse, sex comedies and amorous romances – with a tongue-in-cheek religious metaphor: "She who so well could love's kind passion paint, / We piously believe, must be a saint [...]".[41]

Libertine ethics

The case, in Behn's appreciation, is somewhat different if rakes talk about love, but actually only think of quick sexual gratification. Many of these fictional libertines seem to have no conscience or sense of sin at all, but, like their idols, Hobbes and Lucretius, divorce "morality from any considerations of divine judgement".[42] The speaker in the following poem, for instance, glories in his conquests and subsequent betrayals:

A thousand martyrs I have made,
All sacrificed to my desire;
A thousand beauties have betrayed,
That languish in resistless fire.[43]

In *The Feign'd Curtizans*, too, the rake Galliard derides the idea of faithfulness to one woman only:

Constancy! And wouldst thou have me one of those dull Lovers who believe it their Duty to Love a Woman till her Hair and Eyes change Colour, for fear of the Scandalous Name of an inconstant![...] Let old Age and infirmity bring Repentance- - -there's her feeble Province [...].[44]

Truth and fidelity, in his eyes, are virtues appropriate only for the old and the dumb.[45] He has no scruples about lying, if it will win him a night with a woman; he will swear any number of oaths he never intends to keep: "Nay, Gad if I loose [sic!] a fine wench for want of Oaths [...], the devil's in me."[46] Willmore similarly flouts conventional moral precepts and seems genuinely surprised that a woman

---

40 A. Behn, *A Paraphrase on the Lords Prayer*, in *Works*, Vol. 1, cit., pp. 171–174, p. 173.
41 *Epilogue* to A. Behn, *The Widow Ranter*, in *Works*, Vol. 7, cit., pp. 285–354, p. 354.
42 W. Chernaik, p. 28.
43 A. Behn, *Lycidus*, in *The Works of Aphra Behn*, ed. by J. Todd, Vol. 4, London, Pickering, 1993, pp. 377–421, p. 385.
44 A. Behn, *The Feign'd Curtizans*, in *Works*, Vol. 6, cit., I. 1, pp. 91–92.
45 Cf. W. Chernaik, p. 25.
46 A. Behn, *The Feign'd Curtizans*, in *Works*, Vol. 6, cit., V. 4, p. 154.

like the courtesan Angellica Bianca could actually have believed his false oaths of eternal love: "Broke my Vows! [...] where hast thou liv'd? / Amongst the Gods? for I never heard of mortal Man, / That has not broke a thousand Vows."[47] Being foresworn is simply the way of the world and is not likely to give a man any qualms. Until he is "dull enough to be Religious",[48] he swears, there is little hope he will ever marry. In a contemptuous shrug at middle-class values he makes it clear that he is only interested in women as temporary sexual partners: "[...] why, what the Devil, shou'd I do with a virtuous Woman? [...] Virtue is but an infirmity in Woman; a Disease that renders even the handsome ungrateful [...]."[49] In the end, however, he is won over by the witty and virtuous Hellena after all, whose fortune of 200,000 crowns may well have played a role in his conversion.

Behn, of course, was not the only playwright who made characters express such cynical sentiments. In fact, Galliard's and Willmore's defence of pro-miscuity is strikingly similar to Dorimant's smug refusal to take responsibility for broken oaths in Etherege's *The Man of Mode:* "Constancy at my years! 'Tis not a virtue in season; you might as well expect the fruit the autumn ripens i'the spring."[50] Morality and sober respectability, it is implied, are against human nature, and are only good for those who cannot enjoy the pleasures of life any longer. It is little wonder that clergymen like Jeremy Collier complained about the "Immorality and Profaneness of the English Stage".[51]

Of course the fact that Behn portrayed such characters does not mean that she approved of their morals. As a woman she was well aware of the misogynist ethos of such libertines, and of the double sexual morality of the period, which made it impossible for women to play by the same rules. Yet despite her insight into male egotism and violence in her comedies, she also tends to paint her rakes as charismatic and irresistibly attractive, and, like many male dramatists of her time, invites the audience to be titillated by their exploits and hence to some extent makes it complicit in their deeds.[52]

Most of her clever heroines are well aware of the stringency of social rules – though they may care little about religious ones. They may pretend to be sexually available to attract men, giving them tit for tat: "Unconscionable! constant at my years? / – Oh, t'were to cheat a thousand! / Who, between this and my dull Age of Constancy, / Expect the distribution of my Beauty."[53] However, these witty

47 A. Behn, *The Rover*, in *Works*, Vol. 5, cit., V. 1, p. 513.
48 Ivi, V. 2, p. 500.
49 Ivi, IV. 2, p. 496.
50 G. Etherege, *The Man of Mode*, ed. by J. Barnard, London, A&C Black 1988 [1979], II. 1, p. 47.
51 J. Collier, *A Short View of the Immorality and Prophaneness of the English Stage* (1698).
52 G. Southcombe, cit., p. 157.
53 A. Behn, *The Feign'd Curtizans*, in *Works*, Vol. 6, cit., IV. 1, p. 128.

women know that even rakes will only marry a virgin. Thus, if they remain steadfast in the face of sexual 'temptation', they do so not out of a sense of religious or moral obligation but for the sake of expediency – as Hellena sarcastically observes when Willmore talks to her about free love: "[...] what shall I get? A cradle full of noise and mischief, with a pack of repentance at my back?"[54]

Occasionally, however, Behn also portrays female rakes, who take the same liberties as men to follow their unabashed desires, caring little about their social reputation or marital vows. After having been debauched and deserted by her brother-in-law, Silvia in *Love Letters Between a Nobleman and his Sister* throws all moral rules overboard and unscrupulously exploits other men. Miranda in *The Fair Jilt* falsely accuses a priest of having sexually assaulted her, and later tries to have her sister killed. None of these women, however, meet with 'poetic justice' – on the contrary, they continue to lead comfortable lives, unbothered by a bad conscience and unafraid of divine punishment. Mirtilla in *The Younger Brother* feels as little moral obligation to be faithful as any male libertine: "Why should I lose a Pleasure for a Promise, since Time, that gives our Youth so short a Date, may well excuse our needful Perjury?"[55] She, too, lacks any sense of sin in her doings and remains quite unperturbed by the charge of having broken her love vows; she has simply fallen out of love: "I was a Lover then, shou'd Heav'n concern its self with Lover's Perjuries, 'twou'd find no leisure to preserve the Universe."[56] It is significant that she should choose her maxims from classical antiquity –Horace's "carpe diem"[57] and Ovid's cynical observation that "Jupiter from on high laughs at the perjuries of lovers".[58]

Given the characters' secular thinking, it is perhaps no wonder that the supernatural powers they appeal to are often the gods of classical antiquity, rather than the Christian deity – Gods less strict in amorous matters and themselves involved in diverse love affairs. Pastoral poetry indeed regularly operated with a paraphernalia of Greek and Roman Gods. Especially references to the God of love or the baroque cherubs abound. After the Reformation the figure of Cupid became ubiquitous in English culture.[59] The desires he represented (love's blindness, transience, indiscriminateness, and immoral transgressiveness) were "adversarial" to "the 'erotic politics' of English Protestantism" and its "attempt

---

54 A. Behn, *The Rover*, in *Works*,Vol. 5, cit., V. 1, p. 517.
55 A. Behn, *The Younger Brother*, in *Works*, Vol. 7, cit., V. 3, p. 410.
56 Ivi, II. 2. p. 381.
57 Q. Horacius Flaccus, *Carmina* I. 11. http://www.thelatinlibrary.com/horace/carm1.shtml.
58 P. Ovidius Naso, *Ars Amoria* I. 16. http://www.poetryintranslation.com/PITBR/Latin/Art ofLoveBkI.htm.
59 J. Kingsley-Smith, *Cupid in Early Modern Literature and Culture,* Cambridge, Cambridge University Press, 2010, p. 1.

to separate licit from illicit love".[60] Thus Galliard invites Cornelia: "Come, to thy private Chamber let us haste, / The sacred Temple of the God of Love! / And consecrate thy power",[61] and Laura Lucretia in the same play prays: "Descend, ye little winged Gods of Love [...] ."[62] Willmore, too, (falsely) swears "By all the little Gods of Love",[63] and Bacon in *The Widdow Ranter* talks about the god of love when he is courting the married Indian Queen.[64]

Even incest is excused by some of the rakes with preposterous arguments. In *The Dutch Lover*, a man enamoured with his sister utilizes the double meaning of 'love' as both affection and sexual desire to convince the woman that she is actually at fault for not yielding to his perverse desire: as a sister, she ought to 'love' her sibling. Indeed, he even accuses her of being guilty of murder, because her coyness is 'killing' him. Behn obviously does not condone his behaviour, but she allows the audience to laugh at his pseudo-arguments.

> *Silvio.* Can you believe it sin to love a Brother? it is not so in nature.
> *Cleonte.* Not as a Brother, Sir; but otherwise
> It is, by all the Laws of Men and Heaven.
> *Silvio.* Sister, so 'tis that we should do no murther,
> And yet you daily kill, and I among the number
> Of your victims, must charge you with the sin of
> Killing me, a Lover, and a Brother.[65]

A similar attempt to render incest harmless is made by Philander in *Love Letters Between a Nobleman and his Sister*. In Restoration understanding, a love relationship with his sister-in-law would have counted as incest. In a Hobbesian, "unapologetically egotistical view of self-governance"[66] he makes light of the law and even employs the Bible itself to legitimate sin, by referring to incestuous relationships in the old Testament, which contemporaneous ecclesiastics tried to explain away by the scarcity of humans on earth in these early times (as in the case of Adam's children, or Lot and his daughters). Hence Philander invites his sister-in-law, Silvia:

> [...] let us love like the first race of men, nearest allied to God, promiscuously they lov'd, and possess'st, Father and Daughter, Brother and Sister met, and reap'd the joys of Love

---

60 Ivi, pp. 1, 2 and 5.
61 A. Behn, *The Feign'd Curtizans*, in *Works*, Vol. 6, cit., IV. 2, p. 137.
62 Ivi, V. 2, p. 149.
63 A. Behn, *The Rover*, in *Works*, Vol. 5, cit., I. 2, p. 464.
64 Cf. A. Behn, *Widdow Ranter*, in *Works*, Vol. 7, cit., II. 1, p. 312.
65 A. Behn, *The Dutch Lover*, in *Works*, Vol. 5, cit., pp. 157–238, II. 6, p. 187.
66 C. Tilmouth, *Passion's Triumph over Reason: A History of the Moral Imagination from Spenser to Rochester*, Oxford, Oxford University Press, 2007, p. 213.

without controul, and counted it Religious coupling, and 'twas encourage'd too by Heav'n it self [...].[67]

Such outrageous ethical positions and equivocation were obviously exactly the kind of material that would have been regarded as a blasphemous treatment of Holy Writ by religious believers.

As has been shown above in the case of the female rakes, it is by no means only men who resort to sophistry. In *The History of the Nun* the eponymous protagonist has to decide whether to break her religious vow or give up the man she has fallen in love with. A violated vow, she considers, might be shameful, but, since

> [...] she was born in Sin, and could not live without it; [... and was] Human, and no Angel, [...] that Sin might be as soon forgiven, as another; [...] since all her Devout Endeavours could not defend her from the Cause, Heaven ought to excuse the Effect [...].[68]

In fact, the narrative here taps into a central problem connected with the control of passion: if love is indeed irresistible, as writers of amorous fiction tried to show, lovers can hardly be blamed for their actions when carried away by passions which transgress human and divine law. In the case of Philander or the Nun, Behn realizes well enough that, no matter how fierce their passion, there is still free will and personal responsibility – whatever they might say in their twisted arguments. Less than four decades later, another female writer of love romances equivocates much more strongly on the subject.

> [...] it would be meer [sic!] madness, as well as ill nature, to say a person was blameworthy for what was unavoidable. When love once becomes in our power, it ceases to be worthy of that name; no man really possest [sic!] with it, *can* be master of his actions; and whatever effects it may enforce, are no more to be condemned, than poverty, sickness, deformity, or any other misfortune incident to humane nature."[69]

In such a concept, no sexual transgression could ever be considered a sin, since love is believed to stifle free will; it is interpreted as a compelling stroke of fate – and yet, absurdly, in these eighteenth-century narratives women who 'fall' are promptly punished by divine providence (indeed, much more so than in Behn's more tolerant and liberal understanding).

---

67 A. Behn, *Love Letters Between a Nobleman and His Sister*, in *The Works of Aphra Behn*, ed. by J. Todd, Vol. 2, London, Pickering, 1993, p. 12.

68 A. Behn, *The History of the Nun*, in *Works*, Vol. 2, cit., pp. 205–258, pp. 235–236.

69 E. Haywood, *Love in Excess, or, The Fatal Enquiry*, ed. by D. Oakleaf, Peterborough, ON, Broadview, 2000², pp. 185–186.

Religious denominations and political factions

Up till now, this paper has investigated Restoration free-thinking and its mocking attitude towards religion. However, we need to remember that despite the libertinism and scepticism of court circles and their derision of piety and bigotry, religious conflicts continued to be acerbic in the last decades of the seventeenth century and resulted in factionalism and religious intolerance, though these conflicts were always also linked with power struggles between Parliament and the monarch. The fear that Charles II, who had no legitimate son, would be followed by his unpopular Catholic brother James fuelled a number of political crises in the 1670s and 1680s, including the entirely fictitious Popish Plot supposedly meant to assassinate the king, which resulted in anti-Catholic hysteria throughout the realm; the Exclusion Crisis, in which Whig members of Parliament tried to exclude James from the succession; and the Protestant Rye House Plot to murder James. When James II finally became King after his brother's death in 1685, his ill-advised Declaration of Indulgence, in which he repealed the penal laws against Catholics and Protestant Dissenters, finally led to the Revolution of 1688 and his loss of the throne of England.

Religious conflicts, thus, were linked with political conflicts, and religious belief often was interpreted as political positioning. Behn was a Tory and supporter of James II, and it is intriguing that despite her general scepticism her works occasionally evince an interest in Catholicism. The sympathies she shows for her Spanish or Italian heroines in plays like *The Rover* or *Feign'd Curtizans*, however, have little to do with doctrinal questions, but rather with the characters' wit and resourceful rebellion against forced marriages, and, more generally, perhaps also with a certain sympathy for a culture which was accused by stolid Protestants to regard venereal sin as merely venial.[70] The naïve Englishman Blunt is astonished, in Naples, "With what Order and decency Whoring's Establisht here by Virtue of the Inquisition [...]."[71] Several of her narratives are set in nunneries on the continent, though the subject is never faith itself, but amorous entanglements. If anything, Behn's attraction to Catholicism was aesthetic rather than religious. Thus, the narrator of the amorous novel *Love Letters Between a Nobleman and his Sister* is put into a rapture by the beautiful music during mass, the flowers and incense, the angelic choir and the baroque magnificence of the Church:

> [...] and sure there is nothing gives an Idea of real Heaven, like a Church all adorn'd [..] and Musick, [...] to Ravish the Ear; both which inspire the Soul with unresistable

---

70 G. Southcombe, cit., p. 155.
71 A. Behn, *The Rover,* in *Works*, Vol. 5, cit., II. 2, p. 468.

Devotion [...] and I can Swear for my own part, in those Moments a thousand times I have wish'd to Die [...].[72]

It is indeed characteristic that in this description she blends religious and erotic experience, playing on the double meaning of words like "die", "ravish" or "devotion".

As a rule, in Behn's works, a Church – no matter whether Catholic, Anglican or Nonconformist – is not a place of prayer or spiritual collection, but of flirtation, since it is one of the few public places an upper-class woman could visit unaccompanied, without arousing suspicion. The sprightly heroine Bellemante in *The Emperor of the Moon* confesses to her cousin: "I have been at the chapel, and seen so many beaux, such a number of plumes, I could not tell which I should look on must"; thus, instead of paying her devotion to heaven, she "did nothing but admire its handiwork".[73] Similarly, Laura Lucretia in *The Feign'd Curtizans* did not go "to Church with any other Devotion, but that which warms my heart for my young English Cavalier, whom I hop't to have seen there [...]".[74] No wonder, then, that the jealous old Sir Feeble Fainwood in *The Luckey Chance* wants to forbid his bride to attend a service, arguing that "there are more Cuckolds destin'd at Church than are made out of it."[75] Indeed, while her husband attends a religious meeting at his conventicle, Lady Fancy meets her lover at home, confessing that she "never wished well to long Prayer till this minute."[76] Most shocking of all, in *The Fair Jilt*, the eponymous female protagonist tries to rape (!) the handsome young priest in the very sacristy, under pretence of going to confession.

Nonetheless, Behn in her works rarely joins in the satiric attacks on clergymen, who were frequent targets of scorn and ridicule in Restoration writings – much to the ire of the clergy. Some of Behn's characters occasionally do scoff at clerics in offhand remarks. Willmore names a "Priest and *Hymen*" in one breath with a hangman,[77] and the furious Blunt, having been cheated by a whore, vows to become "as fathless as a Phisitian [sic!], as uncharitable as a Church-man, and as ill-natur'd as a Poet.[78] When one of the cowards in *The Widdow Ranter* pleads the "Benefit of the Clergy", he is told by his interlocutor that he "never knew anybody that ever did benefit by 'em [...]."[79]

Behn's attacks, however, are mainly directed at the Puritans as old (and new)

---

72 A. Behn, *Love Letters Between a Nobleman and his Sister*, in *Works*, Vol. 2, cit., p. 381.
73 A. Behn, *The Emperor of the Moon*, in *Works*, Vol. 7, cit., I. 1, p. 165.
74 A. Behn, *The Feign'd Curtizans*, in *Works*, Vol. 6, cit., I. 1, p. 91.
75 A. Behn, *The Luckey Chance*, in *Works*, Vol. 7, cit., I. 3, p. 233.
76 A. Behn, *Sir Patient Fancy*, in *Works*, Vol. 5, pp. 1–81, IV. 2, p. 54.
77 A. Behn, *The Rover*, in *Works*, Vol. 5, cit., V. 1, p. 517.
78 Ivi, IV. 5, p. 504.
79 A. Behn, *The Widdow Ranter*, in *Works*, Vol. 7, cit., IV. 2, p. 336.

enemies of royal prerogative, who inveigh against supposedly loose morals and reject harmless wit and mirth as sinful. She pits against their hypocritical grumpiness the cavalier – i.e., royalist – ethos, which refuses to regard good living, drinking and a mistress as sinful behaviour. Thus, Sir Anthony defends his nephew's life-style against the criticism of a pseudo-pious Whig:

> What sin, what expences? He wears good Cloaths, why Trades-men get the more by him; he keeps his Coach, 'tis for his ease; a Mistriss, 'tis for his pleasure; he games, 'tis for his diversion: And where's the harm of this?[80]

All her Puritan zealots are painted as hypocrites. Lady Fancy calls the preachers at the conventicle her husband attends "a herd of snivelling, grinning Hypocrites" who secretly pat and grab her lecherously.[81] In *The Roundheads* a supposedly pious Elder recommends himself to Lady Desbro as a discreet would-be lover, as "the Sin lyeth in the Scandal"[82], not in the act of adultery itself. His hypocritical attitude, ironically, is indistinguishable from that of the 'ladies of honour' in the most notorious of all Restoration sex comedies, Wycherley's *The Country Wife*, who likewise guard not their chastity, but only their reputation. Tickletext, a preacher of a London conventicle, affects to hate the Catholic courtesans "worse than beads or holy-water",[83] so he pretends to attempt to convert them to be able to visit them without scandal; in a veritable Hobbesian manner, he then argues that since Roman law allows prostitution, fornication must needs be legal and no sin. Like Tickletext, the zealous Sir Patient Fancy finds "Popish Horn-Pipes and Jesuitical Cymballs" as abominable as organs and anthems.[84] The true reason for Behn's animosity, however, is not his narrow-minded anti-Catholicism, but his political opposition to the Stuarts, which, in her estimate, often went hand in hand with Protestant zeal and bigotry. The title that he, a rich middle-class citizen of London, holds is likely to have been conferred during Cromwell's rule – which would, again, qualify him for Behn's distrust and hatred. Sir Patient, his wife scoffs, is "vainly proud" of "his Rebellious opinion, for his Religion means nothing but that […]."[85]

Though there is little sense of sin being a violation of divine law or religious precepts in Behn's writing, there is a strong sense of loyalty and moral obligation towards the Stuart monarchs. Significantly, it is in a poem to the bishop Burnet, written in answer to his invitation to write a panegyric on William III, who had

---

80 A. Behn, *The City Heiress*, in *Works*, Vol. 7, cit., I. 1, p. 16.
81 A. Behn, *Sir Patient Fancy*, in *Works*, Vol. 5, cit., II. 1, p. 19.
82 A. Behn, *The Roundheads*, in *Works*, Vol. 6, cit., III. 2, p. 395.
83 A. Behn, *The Feign'd Curtizans*, in *Works*,Vol. 6, cit., I. 2, cit., p. 97.
84 A. Behn, *Sir Patient Fancy*, in *Works*, Vol. 5, cit., III. 7, p. 38.
85 Ivi, II. 1, p. 19.

deposed James II, that she explicitly referred to her "conscience", which forbade her to swim with the tide and welcome the new king.[86]

> My Muse that would endeavour fain to glide
> With the fair prosperous gale, and the full driving tide.
> But loyalty commands with pious force,
> That stops me in the thriving course.[87]

Bishop Burnet was the clergyman who had converted Rochester on his deathbed – a conversion Behn had refused to acknowledge in her elegy on her friend. Now, at the end of her life, she regarded Burnet as the propagandistic mastermind justifying to the nation the breach of the oath of allegiance to James; and she refused to play along with what she must have regarded as rank rebellion. Sarcastically she congratulates Burnet on his success: "'Tis to your pen, great Sir, the nation owes / For all the good this mighty change has wrought" – to a pen that made Britons abandon their principles:

> [...] Oh strange effect of a seraphic quill!
> That can by unperceptable degrees
> Change every notion, every principle
> To any form, its great dictator please.[88]

Turning the moral tables on Burnet,[89] she presents him as seducing the unprincipled public[90] and attributes the ascension to the throne "not to the merit of William of Orange, the worthiness of the cause, or even the Will of God,"[91] but to Burnet's print propaganda and political strategies. Although in this poem the word "seraphic" is clearly ironic, the term "pious", for once, is meant dead seriously, in the sense of an inalienable moral obligation to her former king. Her loyalty is not based on hope of a reward after death for her steadfastness, but on a proud sense of personal honour vis a vis the time-servers of the age.

---

86 Cf. W. Chernaik, p. 158.
87 A. Behn, *A Pindaric Poem to the Reverend Doctor Burnet, on the Honour he did me of Enquiring after me and my Muse*, in *Works*, Vol. 1, cit., pp. 307–310, p. 309.
88 Ibidem.
89 M. L. Williamson, *Raising their Voices. British Women Writers, 1650–1750*, Detroit, Wayne State University Press, 1990, p. 144.
90 J. Todd, *The Secret Life of Aphra Behn*, cit., p. 426.
91 P. McDowell, *The Women of Grub Street. Press, Politics and Gender in the London Literary Marketplace 1678–1730*, Oxford, Clarendon Press, 1998, p. 2.

John F. Maune

Godded Coriolanus: Warrior Savior

Introduction

The eponymous character of Shakespeare's late tragedy *Coriolanus*, possibly his last tragedy and Roman play, is a warrior rich in the Roman virtues, if not humility and political acumen. Warren Chernaik wrote, "No play by Shakespeare is more obsessively concerned with Roman values, or more critical of these values, than *Coriolanus*" and that valiantness was the most honoured of all Roman virtues.[1] Coriolanus himself seems rigidly bound to valiantness, but although the paragon of valor, he is seen by almost all who encounter him throughout the play as a haughty peevish patrician who suffers from excessive pride. Wyndham Lewis likened him to "a proud man who assumes the right to despise persons of a lesser breed"[2] which sums up the majority of critical opinions. The play, like the protagonist, is fairly linear, and can be seen to follow the classic mold of hubris leading to tragedy. However, the text, as with most Shakespeare, especially late Shakespeare, supports a wide range of interpretations: "Shakespeare's supreme preoccupation is always with his fable, which explains, and is explained by, human nature in action", and "Shakespeare wrote for the story, not for the moral".[3]

Harold Clarke Goddard saw Coriolanus as one of many "incorrigible truthtellers who discomfort and undo the hypocrites and knaves" that Shakespeare created starting with Hamlet, and noted that Coriolanus and Cordelia both have "Cor" in their names, Latin for heart.[4] Another part of his name that brings forth less flattering imagery of lower body or backward connotations – Coriol-anus –

1 W. Chernaik, *The Myth of Rome in Shakespeare and His Contemporaries*, Cambridge, Cambridge University Press, 2011, pp. 165–166.

2 W. Lewis, *The Lion and the Fox*, London, Grant Richards, 1927, p. 241.

3 M. W. MacCallum, *Shakespeare's Roman Plays and Their Background*, New York, Russell and Russell, 1967, p. 468.

4 H. C. Goddard, *The Meaning of Shakespeare, vol. 2*. 2nd edn., Chicago, University of Chicago Press, 1960, p. 210.

is highlighted by Maurice Hunt.[5] Olivier found Coriolanus to be "a very straightforward, reactionary son of a so-and-so",[6] Fiennes was moved by his "aspiration to unbending purity",[7] and for Andrew Cecil Bradley, Coriolanus was "a noble, even a lovable, being".[8] As with Goddard finding similarities between Cordelia and Coriolanus, it is even possible to find Christ-like attributes in the vituperative man of war.[9]

In this chapter, I will argue that Shakespeare's Coriolanus, though flawed, adhered zealously to six of the seven Christian heavenly virtues, only falling short, monstrously and pitifully so, on patience. Thus, he succumbed – repeatedly and with no compunction – to patience's alternative of the seven deadly sins: wrath. Pride was not at all his undoing, though many in and out of the play, fault him for such. Also, Shakespeare, not one averse to psychological sleights of hand, made the anti-hero Coriolanus in many ways a figurative Christ, though the haughty, cursing, peevish, killing machine Coriolanus and Christ are a very extreme or carnivalesque misalliance.[10]

The worst deadly sin and the chiefest virtue

The seven Christian deadly sins, and their counterpart heavenly virtues, were common themes in religious, dramatic, and literary works and well known to London audiences of the 1600's: morality plays, Chaucer's Canterbury Tales, and Marlowe's Dr. Faustus where they parade across the stage in human form. Though set in Rome with Roman values, the seven deadly sins are continually brought to mind throughout the entire play with the frequent mention of the worst deadly sin – pride (proud) – which is mentioned six times concerning Coriolanus in the first scene alone.

1.1.28 – 31
First Citizen – though soft-conscienced men can be
content to say it was for his country he did it to

---

5 See M. Hunt, *The Backward Voice of Coriol-anus*, in "Shakespeare Studies", 32, 2004, pp. 220–239.

6 J. Cook, *Shakespeare's Players*, 2nd edn., London, Harrap Limited, 1985, p. 94.

7 J. Curry, *Shakespeare on Stage*, London, Nick Hern Books, 2010, pp. 38–39.

8 A. C. Bradley, *Shakespearean Tragedy: Lectures on Hamlet, Othello, King Lear, Macbeth*, 2nd edn., London, Macmillan, 1905, p. 83.

9 See J. Maune, *Topsy-Turvy and Other Carnivalesque Aspects in Coriolanus*, in "Athens Journal of Philology", 2016, pp. 23–38, available from: http://www.athensjournals.gr/philology/2016-3-1-2-Maune.pdf.

10 See J. Maune, *Topsy-Turvy*, cit.

please his mother and to be partly proud; which he
is, even till the altitude of his virtue.[11]

The first citizen in the opening moments succinctly sets the stage for the play; pride and virtue take center stage throughout the drama. Coriolanus is a paragon of virtue; he is a valiant warrior. This undeniable virtue is freely acknowledged by the first citizen, but, he feels, Coriolanus's pride is of similarly grand stature. Also, very damning by Roman standards, his acts of valor are not done in service of his country, but for his mother and to fuel his pride. Referring to his mother, the first citizen brings up pietas, another important Roman virtue of duty or devotion to state, family, and the gods. Thus, the first citizen in backhanded fashion praises Coriolanus while offsetting the compliment. Though Coriolanus disparages the many-head beast which has lead various critics to label Shakespeare a classist, the plebeians are actually "presented with both complexity and sympathy"[12] as expressive individuals.[13] When we first meet Coriolanus, at that time still Marcius,[14] he does little to suggest the first citizen has misspoken.

> 1.1.153 – 166
> **Coriolanus** – Thanks. What's the matter, you dissentious rogues,
> That, rubbing the poor itch of your opinion,
> Make yourselves scabs?
> **First Citizen** – We have ever your good word.
> **Coriolanus** – He that will give good words to thee will flatter
> Beneath abhorring. What would you have, you curs,
> That like nor peace nor war? the one affrights you,
> The other makes you proud. He that trusts to you,
> Where he should find you lions, finds you hares;
> Where foxes, geese: you are no surer, no,
> Than is the coal of fire upon the ice,
> Or hailstone in the sun. Your virtue is
> To make him worthy whose offence subdues him
> And curse that justice did it.

The tribunes – penned as calculating and duplicitous, or model Machiavellians – echo this sentiment too, in private of course, stressing his pride and alluding to his valor.

---

11 All quotes from the play are from the following source: W. Shakespeare, *Coriolanus*, K. Deighton, (ed.), London, Macmillan, 1900, available from: http://www.shakespeare-online.com/plays/corio_1_2.html.

12 J. Dollimore, *Radical Tragedy*, Chicago, University of Chicago Press, 1984, p. 224.

13 A. Leggatt, *Shakespeare's Political Drama*, London, Routledge, 1988, pp. 197, 201.

14 Coriolanus will be used throughout this paper even in scenes before he had become Coriolanus.

1.1.247–253
Brutus – The present wars devour him: he is grown
Too proud to be so valiant.
Sicinius – Such a nature,
Tickled with good success, disdains the shadow
Which he treads on at noon: but I do wonder
His insolence can brook to be commanded
Under Cominius.

However, the tribunes read Coriolanus's intentions through their own dissolute standards; they feel he must covet the immense political power inherent in being consul (2.3.155–157) and feel it beneath his proud stature to serve under Cominius. The tribunes are glaringly wrong. Coriolanus never wanted the consulship and is noticeably relieved to escape his political service, even at the price of banishment,[15] and is unwaveringly loyal, the Roman virtue pietas, to Cominius. Anne Barton discusses the influence of Machiavelli on *Coriolanus*[16] though Coriolanus abhors political intrigue and lying; he is an antithetical prince. Volumnia says he is "too absolute" (3.2.51) and guileless, while Menenius acknowledges that "his heart's his mouth" (3.1.322). Volumnia raised him to be the soldier he became and loaded him with Roman precepts, but her success was her failure. He took her teachings to absolutes that she never intended. She saw Roman virtue as a means to an end while her son took them as the end itself: serve not for personal gain, that includes pride, but merely as it is right to do so. Volumnia raised a fanatic. She repeatedly tries to get him to lie for, in her opinion, his own sake to become consul (3.2.23–27, 51–57, 60–65, 67–84, 89–103), but he will have none of it.

Her advice in act 3, scene 2 to dissemble and fawn is not at all honorable or public spirited, as she is merely thinking of having her son obtain the office. Once consul he can summarily do as he pleases with the rabble plebeians with her blessing as they will then be powerless to stop him.[17] Coriolanus stands firm saying that he will not buy the people's mercy, thus the consulship, for one fair word (3.3.114). He is painfully, to others and himself, honest – the Roman virtue

---

15 See J. Maune, *Topsy-Turvy*, cit.
16 See A. Barton, *Essays, Mainly Shakespearean*, Cambridge, Cambridge University Press, 1994, pp. 136–160.
17 J. Dollimore says that "Volumnia conceives of virtus not as essence but as political strategy" which seems to render the meaning, its essence perhaps, of the word virtue as devoid of moral or ethical boundaries. He further extols Volumnia for her "understanding that power is something to be appropriated", because following her success saving Rome she is the most powerful person in Rome. He supports, at least for Coriolanus and Volumnia, that a public figure do and say whatever it takes, that is dissemble, to appropriate power. Such strategy worked well for Donald Trump to become the 45th U.S. president. J. Dollimore, *Radical Tragedy*, cit., pp. 218–230.

veritas – not desirable in a politician. Volumnia knows her son can still easily become consul, which she greatly desires, so she tries another of his many buttons[18] and comments on his pride in a stern rebuke.

> 3.2.153–154
> **Volumnia** – Thy valiantness was mine, thou suck'dst it from me,
> But owe thy pride thyself.

Coriolanus holds pride in contempt which he states in the opening scene in his first tirade (1.1.157–177). Volumnia knows it all too well. She is trying to ma-nipulate Coriolanus by shaming him or rousing his anger similar to what the tribunes and Aufidius do later in the play. Unlike her son, Volumnia has "a brain that leads her use of anger to better vantage" (3.2.38–39).

The seven deadly sins

Volumnia is willing to take credit for her son's virtue but not for his perceived pride. Coriolanus is singled out for his pride, while other characters personify various deadly sins.

The tribunes' and Volumnia's insight is occluded by their own thirst for power – the deadly sin of greed. Aufidius too puts his desire for power above his honor. The second citizen, "you must in no way say he is covetous" (1.1.34) and Cominius, "he covets less than misery itself would give" (2.2.143–144), both attest to Coriolanus's lack of greed. However, his refusal of one-tenth of the spoils of Corioli (1.9.37–46) quite strongly shows his disinterest in material gains.

Lust and sexual imagery are present, but are portrayed in the play in an off-centered way. The first sexual reference is uttered by Coriolanus, but is subdued and G-rated.

> 1.6.39–42
> **Coriolanus** – O, let me clip ye
> In arms as sound as when I woo'd, in heart
> As merry as when our nuptial day was done,
> And tapers burn'd to bedward!

We first meet Volumnia in a quaint domestic scene where she is affably sewing with Coriolanus's wife Virgilia. This is in stark contrast to the first words out of her mouth in the play. To make her point that honor is the ultimate goal in life, she uses the incestuous image of copulating with her son Coriolanus.

---

18 See J. Maune, *Revealing Tells, Bawdy and Otherwise, in Coriolanus*, in "Athens Journal of Humanities and Arts X Y", 2016, pp. 1–15.

1.3.1–18
Volumnia – I pray you, daughter, sing; or express yourself in a
more comfortable sort: if my son were my husband, I
should freelier rejoice in that absence wherein he
won honour than in the embracements of his bed where
he would show most love.

There is also the homoerotic imagery used by Aufidius when he accepts Coriolanus into his home and country.

4.5.125–129 [104–139]
Aufidius – I have nightly since
Dreamt of encounters 'twixt thyself and me;
We have been down together in my sleep,
Unbuckling helms, fisting each other's throat,
And waked half dead with nothing.

If Aufidius smoked, he would now have his post-coital cigarette while his paramour Coriolanus lay beside him.

The third citizen prior to meeting Coriolanus dressed in the gown of humility says, "we are to put our tongues into those wounds and speak for them" (2.2.5–6). Such allegorical use of the people's tongues is grotesque and even sexual as a kind of cunnilingus, or if Coriolanus's wounds are stigmata, sacrilegious.[19]

Coriolanus first greets Virgilia as his "gracious silence" (2.1.175), which is how their marriage is portrayed. In the intercession scene, his fidelity or control of lust, is made clear: "that kiss I carried from thee, dear; and my true lip hath virgin'd it e'er since" (5.3.50–52).

Gluttony is personified by Menenius. He cannot speak a few lines without referencing food or its anus dependent end products.[20] His telling of the famous fable of the body rebelling against the belly in the opening scene is self-referential to his own infatuated relation with his belly. He relates Coriolanus's faults talking of meal and bran (3.1.401–404), and before approaching Coriolanus to dissuade him from sacking Rome, he puts great store in pleading with Coriolanus only after he is well fed (5.1.56–67). Charney, along with disease and animals, thinks food imagery is a dominating motif of the play.[21]

Volumnia parodies the belly fable into a self-negating gluttony where her greed and wrath consume herself.

---

19 See J. Maune, *Topsy-Turvy*, cit.
20 See J. Maune, *Revealing Tells*, cit.
21 M. Charney, *Shakespeare's Roman Plays: The Function of Imagery in the Drama*, Cambridge, Harvard University Press, 1963, p. 142.

4.2.65–67
Menenius – And, by my troth, you have cause. You'll sup with me?
Volumnia – Anger's my meat; I sup upon myself,
And so shall starve with feeding.

In a sense Volumnia has supped on herself her whole life. She has sent her son off to war to feed her social and political ambitions which she values beyond the measure of his life.

1.3.19–25
Virgilia – But had he died in the business, madam; how then?
Volumnia – Then his good report should have been my son; I
therein would have found issue. Hear me profess
sincerely: had I a dozen sons, each in my love
alike and none less dear than thine and my good
Marcius, I had rather had eleven die nobly for their
country than one voluptuously surfeit out of action.

Her callous and exploitive regard for her son's well-being is reminiscent of Lady MacBeth discussing dashing out the brains of her own baby if necessary to keep her "good" word.

The abjectly immoral tribunes stand in for sloth, envy, greed, and pride. They spend their time tricking or herding (2.1.93) the plebeian pawns to do their bidding. Their ambition is geared toward their own ends, not at all in service to the people;[22] they would be patricians themselves. They envy Coriolanus his fame and good fortune, and worry he will exploit his post with Cominius as they would surely do. After Coriolanus is banished, Brutus suggests they act humbler (4.2.5). Such humbler posturing is attributed to Coriolanus as he has cause to be proud, while Brutus really does play humble as he is proud, though he has cause to be ashamed.

Aufidius succumbs to envy as he sees Coriolanus's stature rise to occlude his own. When Rome is spared, Aufidius only thinks of how he can topple Coriolanus to gain back his "former fortune" (5.3.221). Like the tribunes, Aufidius justifies his assassination of Coriolanus imagining slights that never took place (5.6.24–46).

Coriolanus does wax eloquent and hyperbolic praising Aufidius as a respected enemy. "I sin in envying his nobility, and were I any thing but what I am, I would wish me only he," and "he is a lion that I am proud to hunt" (1.1.220–222, 226–227).

---

22 A. Leggatt, *Shakespeare's Political Drama*, cit., p. 197.

Proud me no prouds

Being called proud by the plebeians, tribunes, Aufidius, his own mother, and Menenius when cornered by the tribunes, is not the same as actually being proud. Olivier said that "Coriolanus's pride is of the nature that he is too proud even to accept praise".[23] Had Coriolanus agreed with all the praise given him and basked in its glory, that too would mean he was proud. Such judgement is grossly unfair setting up a damned if you do and damned if you don't scenario, which occurs again when he is supposed to show his wounds to the people. Everyone but Coriolanus is proud of his wounds. Volumnia and Menenius gush proudly reciting his litany of wounds and how "he has more cause to be proud" (2.1.143). However, much cause he has, Coriolanus is not proud of his wounds which he states again and again (1.9.32–33, 2.2.79–80, 89–91, 157–161, 169–171) – to no avail. He is damned like Cassandra to speak the truth, but not believed. For Jonathan Dollimore "Coriolanus' pride in his wounds is inextricably bound up with the fact that he got them in the same battle where he saw the plebeians run from the noise of our own drums".[24] This is another Catch-22; he is seen as proud if he shows his wounds, and proud if he doesn't. It is easy to prove something when all evidence supports your bias. What of Coriolanus's refusal of a tenth of the spoils of Corioli? He says I "stand upon my common part with those that have beheld the doing" (1.9.45–46). Is this an example of greed? Pride again? Nonsense.

The plebeians are not very adept at asking, and Coriolanus easily dupes them; he neither shows them his wounds, nor "brags unto them, thus I did and thus" (2.2.173). Had he shown his wounds and bragged, would that have also indicated pride? Perhaps he really would "rather have his wounds to heal again than hear say how [he] got them" (2.2.79–80). The same is true when his mother, Cominius, or Titus Lartius try to praise him; he is humble, and would rather not bathe in their words of glory. The tribunes claim he will use his service under Cominius craftily (1.1.260–267), but he shows only deference towards Cominius, vowing to serve him to the best of his ability (1.9.75–80). Coriolanus is uncomfortable and tries to deflect the praise for his heroic deeds in Corioli: "Sir, praise me not; my work hath yet not warm'd me: fare you well" (1.5.18–19), "I have done as you have done; that's what I can; induced as you have been; that's for my country" (1.9.18–20), "I have some wounds upon me, and they smart to hear themselves

---

23 J. Cook, *Shakespeare's Players*, cit., p. 94.
24 This is used to support identity being dependent on social relations. He also wrote that Coriolanus's identity is located in Rome and is close to anomie when he enters Antium. I think Coriolanus had strengthened his identity after the duplicity of his mother and the patricians was exposed. He became more his own man when he broke with his mother and the state. Both were using Coriolanus for their own aims. J. Dollimore, *Radical Tragedy*, cit., pp. 220–222.

remember'd" (1.9.32–33), and "You shout me forth in acclamations hyperbolical; as if I loved my little should be dieted in praises sauced with lies" (1.9.56–59). Upon his flourish-filled return to Rome he does not seek the limelight: "No more of this; it does offend my heart: pray now, no more" (2.1.164–165).

Cominius praises the valor of Coriolanus in detail (2.2.97–137). He is proud of his warrior, but never labels Coriolanus as proud, rather tells him "too modest are you" (1.9.60), and bestows the honorific Coriolanus as Rome must know the value of her own (1.9.24–25).

Coriolanus speaks his mind – following the virtue of honesty, not out of pride – without any concern for consequence which is not socially or politically savvy. "He has been bred i' the wars since he could draw a sword, and is ill school'd in bolted [refined] language" (3.1.401–403). He speaks ill of the plebeians because he was raised to look down on them (3.2.8–14) and he thinks them hares and geese – cowards who shirk their martial obligations "even when the naval of the state was touch'd" (3.1.156). He speaks ill of the tribunes because he thinks them liars and rabble rousers. This is not slander as the plebeians do shirk their martial obligations and the tribunes are lying rabble rousers. Roman virtue is a way of life for Coriolanus, and, in his absolute and not so humble mind, should be true for all Romans.

Two passages give insight into his simple resolute, and immature, character: after single-handedly taking Corioli when he seeks recruits to continue the battle, and after he has waxed vitriolic lambasting the tribunes and plebeians.

1.6.86–94
Coriolanus – If any such be here –
As it were sin to doubt – that love this painting
Wherein you see me smear'd; if any fear
Lesser his person than an ill report;
If any think brave death outweighs bad life
And that his country's dearer than himself;
Let him alone, or so many so minded,
Wave thus, to express his disposition,
And follow Marcius.

3.1.320–325
Menenius – His nature is too noble for the world:
He would not flatter Neptune for his trident,
Or Jove for's power to thunder. His heart's his mouth:
What his breast forges, that his tongue must vent;
And, being angry, does forget that ever
He heard the name of death.

There's the rub. Coriolanus believes and lives by his motivational speech. The same cannot be said for anyone. Coriolanus alone – often angry too. Menenius links his honesty and wrath which are the tragic flaws that unseat him. Coriolanus merely honest is crude, while combined with anger, insufferable. His haughty disdain for the plebeians and their tribunes and ill school'd and abusive language only exacerbate his problems. Fiennes called him "one of the hardest characters to like".[25] He does have cause to be proud which makes it so easy for others – that includes a multitude of critics – to see pride no matter how he behaves. His contemnible less than humble attitude toward the minnows and their Triton(s) (3.1.116) is based on anger over their abuse, as he perceives it, of Roman values – not pride in his own virtues. His behavior with Cominius and Titus Lartius is one of deference and respect for his betters, to serve the Roman state – not pride. He really does view his battlefield actions as nothings (2.2.91) – nothing to do with pride; all to do with Roman virtue.

Coriolanus states the dramatic crux of the whole play and gives deeper insight into his character when he begs for the life of a prisoner in Corioli.

> 1.9.88–98
> **Coriolanus** – The gods begin to mock me. I, that now
> Refused most princely gifts, am bound to beg
> Of my lord general.
> **Cominius** – Take't; 'tis yours. What is't?
> **Coriolanus** – I sometime lay here in Corioli
> At a poor man's house; he used me kindly:
> He cried to me; I saw him prisoner;
> But then Aufidius was within my view,
> And wrath o'erwhelm'd my pity: I request you
> To give my poor host freedom.
> **Cominius** – O, well begg'd!

Wrath 'o'erwhelm'd' his pity. Anger overwhelmed his mercy. Beg and poor are repeated so the audience do not miss their significance. Coriolanus is begging for a poor man – a poor man and a resident of a rebellious city whose hospitality he had accepted in the past. This poignant moment, not even a minute, provides another glimpse into the man and gives insight into his banishment and final act of forgiveness in the intercession scene. He does not despise the plebeians for being poor and powerless. He does not refuse to plead for the consulship because he is unable to beg. He will beg for what he deems worthy, regardless of stature or citizenship: the plunder of war, political power, status, and ignoble life are not worthy. During his banishment, he is overwhelmed by anger that smolders until he decides, like his mother, to make anger his meat and dine with his enemy

---

25 J. Curry, *Shakespeare on Stage*, cit., p. 39.

Aufidius and offer his revengeful services. His anger is with Rome, his thankless birthplace that he now hates (4.4.27). Hating Rome and placing his love on the enemy town of Antium is not at all contradictory or absurd as Dollimore thinks.[26] Coriolanus was banished from Rome and learned the patricians (his mother too) swayed with circumstance. With his blood and heart, he had served Rome valiantly for many years, but the dastard nobles forsook him (4.5.66–103). Of course, he hates Rome, and hopes to enact his revenge.

Before the gates of Rome camps the Volscian army under Coriolanus. There is no hope of defending the city. Cominius goes first to plead with his former soldier: "I minded him how royal 'twas to pardon when it was less expected" (5.1.20–21). He relates how "his injury the gaoler to his pity" (5.1.76–77); his wrath keeps his mercy bound. Menenius leaves to ask forgiveness for Rome from his onetime son, after which Cominius says that Menenius will fail, but only Volumnia and Virgilia have a chance. Coriolanus tries to be stern when meeting with Menenius, but twice talks of his love for Menenius and gives him a letter (5.2.93–97). Menenius is sent away unsated. The strain on Coriolanus is apparent as he is struggling to keep his plans of revenge and destruction unaltered. He doubts his resolve and repeatedly tells Aufidius how unbending he is and how well he is serving his new superiors; "this last old man whom with a crack'd heart I have sent to Rome, loved me above the measure of a father; nay, godded me" (5.3.10–13). Whose heart? Coriolanus wants to say Menenius left with a cracked heart, but his ambiguous sentence structure (fourth type of ambiguity[27]) exposes that his heart too is cracked. Cominius and Menenius had more effect on the god Mars than they realized. He says he will hear no more suits: his resolve nigh broken. His wife, child, and mother arrive and complete the deal melting his anger and freeing his mercy. He knows this time his merciful action will prove most mortal to him.[28]

Shakespeare was not gentle with extremists on either end of the spectrum. As stated earlier from Chernaik, "No play by Shakespeare is more obsessively concerned with Roman values, or more critical of these values, than *Coriolanus*".[29] Coriolanus with his rigid honesty is pure, but is also extremely foolish and easily fooled. The tribunes and Aufidius know how to enrage him, so with minimal effort they do. The tribunes and Aufidius know quite well that Cor-

---

26 J. Dollimore, *Radical Tragedy*, cit., p. 221.

27 W. Empson, *Seven Types of Ambiguity*, New York, New Directions, 1947, p. 133.

28 Not surprisingly Dollimore asserts that the intercession success lies almost completely with Volumnia, Menenius is not mentioned, and Coriolanus's unusual behavior is due to reconstructing his identity and reputation. Goddard suggests that Coriolanus was won over when he saw his wife. Cf J. Dollimore, *Radical Tragedy*, cit, p. 221; H. Goddard, *The Meaning of Shakespeare*, cit., pp. 219–225.

29 W. Chernaik, *The Myth of Rome*, cit., p. 165.

iolanus is a great man, but his strength is also his weakness. Manipulating someone honest to a fault does not require great skill. It matters little that Marc Antony respects honorable Brutus. Brutus, Cordelia, and Coriolanus do not play their zealous devotion to their own honesty with good results: they all die. They look naive and foolish in their virtuous rigidity, and could have avoided their fates by being less absolute and more human.

Coriolanus the Christ

The seven deadly sins were not the only Christian aspects in the play; Shakespeare, not one averse to psychological sleights of hand, made the anti-hero Coriolanus in many ways a figurative Christ. The haughty, cursing, peevish, killing machine Coriolanus and Christ are strange bedfellows: a carnivalesque misalliance.[30]

Marcius the anti-hero antichrist enters Corioli alone, and is presumed dead by his camp who are in the midst of eulogizing him when he appears bloodied like a baby from the womb. Coriolanus the Christ undergoes a simultaneous virginal birth and resurrection, the joining of death and birth, to start the topsy-turvy misalliance. He is reborn again shortly thereafter when given his new name – Coriolanus. Christ died freeing Barabbas, while Coriolanus lived to free the poor man in Corioli. Christ asks God his father to spare him from the crucifixion, to pass the cup, while Coriolanus beseeches the patricians to avoid his upcoming ordeal of pleading for the people's voices (2.2.157–161). Both go to their crucifixions meanly attired. Christ received his wounds dying on the cross for the sins of humanity: dying so all could achieve everlasting life. Each of Coriolanus's 27 gashes was an enemy's grave: Coriolanus living so that others may die. The third citizen talks of the people's tongues in Coriolanus's wounds/stigmata (2.3.5–6) – more profane misalliance. The Bible sees the people condemn Christ their savior by shouting for Barabbas, while the shouts of the Roman citizens cause their city's savior, Coriolanus, to be banished. Thus, ensues the temptation of Coriolanus. He roams beyond the walls of Rome, not the desert, and fights with his own devil: wrath. He also has to confront his zealous virtues; he finds himself with no one to serve. Christ is tested for 40 days, but withstands the devil's temptations – he will be crucified to cleanse the world of sin. Coriolanus gives in to his wrath, and sets his heart to either die by Aufidius's hand, or take his revenge on Rome. Coriolanus will live so others may die. Christ was a god made incarnate – the prince of peace, while Coriolanus was a man who became a god – Mars, the god of war, to fight against his homeland leading a foreign power. The

---

30 See J. Maune, *Topsy-Turvy*, cit.

first supper with the Volscian nobles sees Coriolanus betray Rome, while at the last supper Christ is betrayed by Judas. Christ pleads with God his father to call off the crucifixion, to pass the cup. Coriolanus does not plead to anyone as he is the god, and forgiveness must come from him. Coriolanus the god is entreated by his friends and family to not sack Rome. Here he thinks on his cup, but not to his father he calls out – "O mother, mother!" (5.3.199). He knows the scene is unnatural (5.3.201). He is no god. He does love. His nature is finally pierced; mercy overcomes his anger. His fate is set, and his time as the god Mars ends along with his wrath. He then drinks with his family for his real last supper, as he also did after begging for the poor man's life in Corioli, in holy communion for his benevolence, and also to reassert his return of physical needs as a human when he is most humane. Christ went to Gethsemane knowing he would be arrested and crucified, and Coriolanus went to Antium knowing his fate. Christ was ridiculed and abused while carrying his cross to the crucifixion site where he forgave his executioners. Coriolanus was triumphantly received in Antium as a hero, but his anger again betrays himself as he inflames the people with gibes and insults.

Discussion

Coriolanus was a reactionary son of a so-and-so (so Volumnia is the bitch that Olivier did not name), but he was a virtuous Roman one. His major faults were openly displayed for all to see and child's play to take advantage of: his honesty was too absolute. His wrath was ever to the fore when dealing with the plebeians; he held them in open contempt. However, the people were astute in many matters and saw well into his character.

> 2.2.7–15
> **Second Officer** – Faith, there had been many great men that have
> flattered the people, who ne'er loved them; and there
> be many that they have loved, they know not
> wherefore: so that, if they love they know not why,
> they hate upon no better a ground: therefore, for
> Coriolanus neither to care whether they love or hate
> him manifests the true knowledge he has in their
> disposition; and out of his noble carelessness lets
> them plainly see't.

Coriolanus does not care how the people or tribunes view him. His noble carelessness is his unchecked wrath and honesty – he honors his own truth (3.2.144) however wrong it may be. He behaves like a beast, especially when goaded: traitor or boy of tears. Falling to such taunts is childish. He meets

Aufidius and upbraids him mercilessly; "I do hate thee worse than a promise-breaker" (1.8.1–2). This is his greatest slur – more fit for a schoolboy, than a leader of men. Though a great man, he is a boy in many respects. As children age, most learn to question their own beliefs, and judge consequences and temper their language for social harmony, or on less lofty levels, personal gain and power. Not Coriolanus.

For Dollimore this play supports that individuals are bounded or defined by society.[31] Society does pointedly constrain the other characters, but this play is emphatically concerned with godded Coriolanus. He is immersed in the political turmoil at the start of the republic, but he is not at all political. He lives by his virtues which in Rome were strongly centered on military service of which he was supremely accomplished. Not even his detractors would deny this. He was alone. Coriolanus alone. With a word or a nod of his head he could have become consul, or destroyed Rome. The choice was his alone to make. A cultural materialistic reading of the play finding Coriolanus's stature or identity bound by the patricians or people is forced and absurd. If interpreting it as a classically defined tragedy is out of favor, so be it. It was a drama: an allegorical tale of a great, but flawed man. It was written that way. It was not written with any moral message, just a dramatic story.[32]

I feel that untold critics have identified the flaw incorrectly. Similar to Haydn's joke, Opus 33 N. 2, where the audience is intentionally misled, it appears Shakespeare misled his audience getting everyone to focus on pride, the worst of the seven deadly sins and the favored tragic flaw. The poor man taken prisoner in Corioli whose freedom he begs for is a minor incident of major import. Coriolanus will beg for a poor man, but only when his anger eases can he access his mercy – when his bestial rage is tamed by his humane mercy.

He was brought up to honor the gods, his mother, and superiors, as well as to hold the plebeians in contempt compared to the ruling elite (3.2.8–14). His blind servitude to his mother and the patricians ends during his banishment when he sees they root their honor in expediency, gain, and self-preservation. Coriolanus does bend his honor somewhat when he enters Antium in mean apparel, disguised with face muffled "lest thy wives with spits and boys with stones in puny battle slay me" (4.5.5–6). This recalls Volumnia's words when trying to convince him if in war it is honorable "to seem the same you are not for your best ends", then it should hold true in times of peace (3.2.60–65). As with begging for the poor man, Coriolanus will disguise himself if he sees fit to do so. He doesn't fear death in the least, just an ignoble one.

Coriolanus may sound proud when in his first soliloquy he questions his need to

---

31 See J. Dollimore, *Radical Tragedy*, cit., pp. 218–230.
32 M. W. MacCallum, *Shakespeare's Roman Plays and Their Background*, cit., p. 468.

beg what he deserves of the people – the consulship (2.3.112–124). However, he is most deserving, so for him to state that is, especially to himself, honest, not proud. He has no desire to become consul, but it is the customary course following his valiant martial service. It is also what his mother and his supporters had intended for him for many years. Here the societal factions of the people/tribunes and Volumnia/patricians are pulling him in opposite directions; one wishes him consul, the other not. His trial as a traitor and banishment could be viewed, as Dollimore would, as Coriolanus bounded by society. However, not becoming consul is exactly what Coriolanus desired. Swaying with the senators in the political arena was never his goal (2.1.210). His wrath spent and free from a consulship he never wanted, he is well content before leaving the gates of the city. He even shows compassion doing his best to console those he is leaving. He is gladly leaving his world behind to be a lonely dragon (4.1.33) – a beast on his own terms.

The temptation of Coriolanus sees him to Antium where he will do the Volscians service or die. Here it is possible to see his self-identity having been lost outside the gates of Rome, albeit briefly. He was brought up to serve, not to wander. His service with the Volscians will see him godded by his former enemies whose families he had slain in previous campaigns. His nameless identity is outside the bounds of mortal men.

His final scene in Antium is a replay of his banishment from Rome. Coriolanus is furious that Aufidius could betray him: abhorrent to Coriolanus, especially in one who had earned his respect. Coriolanus knew beforehand that some mortal subterfuge was coming, but he was still incensed being called a traitor and boy of tears. Manipulated again. Raging beast again. Coriolanus denounces Aufidius's accusations as a lie in rapid succession during his final abusive melt down – liar, lie, lie, false, [if] true, 5.6.121–132). He is killed by the conspirators. Is this an honorable death?

In the other Roman plays *Julius Caesar* and *Antony and Cleopatra*, suicide is the noble Roman way, and occurs in pairs of major and minor characters: Cassius and Titinius, Brutus and Portia, Antony and Eros, and Cleopatra and Charmian.[33] There is much death alluded to in *Coriolanus*, but it all takes place offstage. The only death the audience witnesses is Coriolanus's. Taken in a Christian context, his Christlike death must be honorable.

5.6.130–135
Coriolanus – Cut me to pieces, Volsces; men and lads,
Stain all your edges on me. Boy! false hound!
If you have writ your annals true, 'tis there,
That, like an eagle in a dove-cote, I

---

33 M. Charney, *Shakespeare's Roman Plays*, cit., p. 209.

> Flutter'd your Volscians in Corioli:
> Alone I did it. Boy!

In no uncertain terms, he is asking for it: "Cut me to pieces", and "Stain your edges on me." His death can be seen as honorable in the Roman sense if seen as a suicide. He tells the crowd to take their swords to him. Even after this, only the conspirators, not the commoners, kill him. The unparalleled soldier goes down without a fight. His death can be seen as an ancient version of suicide by cop – suicide by mob.[34]

Chernaik quotes Aristotle's axiom: "He who is unable to live in society, or who has no need because he is sufficient for himself, must be either a beast or a god".[35] The pendulous sword Coriolanus shape shifts back and forth from beast to human, and finally to nameless god, then the unnatural scene ends as he accepts he is most mortal to die Christlike for those he loved (5.3.201–207 where mortal presages his death, but also alludes to his loss of godlike status). Mercy and forgiveness leading to eternal life. The gates open to a world elsewhere.

---

34 See J. Maune, *Topsy-Turvy*, cit.
35 W. Chernaik, *The Myth of Rome*, cit., p. 183.

Ibrahim A. El-Hussari

Sense of Guilt: A Freudian Approach to Joseph Conrad's *Heart of Darkness*

The story

Joseph Conrad's *Heart of Darkness* portrays two white men caught in a European colonial experience in the heart of the African continent. It is the story of the German Kurtz, an executive agent for a European corporate ivory company based in Brussels, told by two narrators. The first narrator, an unnamed member of the crew aboard the yacht *Nellie* heading for Africa, frames the story as a detached observer. The second narrator, the protagonist of the internal tale, the young British Charlie Marlow, tells the story as an observer-participant-commentator who starts to feel terribly guilty as he unconsciously admits his timid complicity with Kurtz just before the tale comes to a halt and closes.

After shipping ivory from Africa to Europe for a while, Kurtz suddenly stops this business and is heard of no more. The company sends Charlie Marlow to collect information about the allegedly missing Kurtz. Infatuated with the heroic image of Kurtz without ever seeing him, the tyro Marlow accepts the errand only to see himself undergoing a series of weird situations which provoke him to keep raising questions and to gradually and unintentionally learn about evil and sin while navigating up River Congo in search of his idol, Kurtz.

It all starts at the first station, the coastal station by the mouth of River Congo. Marlow, still onboard the *Nellie*, tacitly takes note of the French cruiser shelling the African continent to "scare dark ghosts", as told by some members of the crew. At the middle station, where the European ivory company's business office is located, Marlow learns a bit more about the White man being enmeshed in the African jungle. There, he comes across a number of contradictory pamphlets written by Kurtz. One of those pamphlets entitled "Exterminate the Brutes" adds to Marlow's suspicion about the journey he is taking and keeps his rosy anticipation of Kurtz in check. At the last or the innermost station, which is the darkest spot in the jungle, Marlow and Kurtz meet as a Freudian double, and the story begins to melt into a nightmare which prompts Marlow to question Kurtz's mission altogether and eventually envision a moral discovery.

The dwelling place of Kurtz, the hut, is located in the farthest spot of the Congolese jungle, in the heart of darkness. It is decorated with human skulls and guarded by warriors: some naked, others half-naked African women and men. Inside the hut, Kurtz is found lying down on the wooden floor, physically weak, terribly sick and a dying man. However, in the presence of Marlow, who has already succeeded to lodge the dying Kurtz back in the cabin, the latter makes a confession through a whisper. He only breathes out a double word "The horror! The horror!" that implies some sort of moral vision – a confession perhaps; then he dies. Fearing he would eventually become another Kurtz if he stayed long in Africa, Marlow decides to break free and sail back to Europe – assumingly to tell the truth about Kurtz.

In Europe, however, Marlow only manages to go about the truth and pass the buck. One year after his return to Europe, and during his visit to the "Intended", Kurtz's fiancée, to deliver Kurtz's personal effects to her for memory, Marlow sees a sad woman in black, still in mourning over the loss of Kurtz and what he symbolizes for her. Touched by the sight of the sorrowful lady and the great image she has patiently painted of Kurtz, Marlow finds himself offering her his 'warm' condolences but swerving from telling the truth. When she asks him to tell her about the last word spoken by Kurtz on his death bed, Marlow hides the truth and tells her a big lie: "The last word he pronounced was – your name."[1]

The moment he tells the lie, he feels guilty of covering up for Kurtz. In fact, Marlow has intentionally replaced the last word Kurtz breathed out while dying. He has replaced Kurtz's "the horror" with his "your name". Only then does Marlow crumble from within, for he feels he is no less sinful than Kurtz. As an unintentional accomplice and secret sharer of Kurtz, Marlow seems to undergo a severe sense of guilt which compels him to make a dumbfounding confession through an unconscious loud thinking through which Kurtz's last word rings up again: "The horror! The horror!"[2]

Sin and guilt: a review

Since the dawn of history, man has been trying to define the purpose of his existence by creating some sort of socio-moral structure and value system to abide by. Within this system lies the purposeful existence of human race and the various assignments prescribed thereof in the service of that purpose. Myths, religions (both polytheistic and monotheistic), community life (both nomadic and civilized) and other forms and shapes of human devices brought up by

---

1 J. Conrad, *Heart of Darkness,* London, Penguin, 1973, p. 110.
2 Ibidem.

various schools of thought across history – all have been put into effect, re-activated, modified, improved, reinterpreted and even replaced in order to keep the endurable momentum of human existence and punish unacceptable trans-gression.

A cluster of negative terms related to human transgression of code as set by various communities, cultures and civilizations has been observed at different paces over ages. Hence the controversy over the issue of sin as a type of trans-gression, for our basic approach to sin remains a litany of personal discomfiture in the first place. Various readings of the term sin emanate from religions and different schools of thought including ethics, philosophy, law and literature. However, they all consider that sin and guilt do conflate for the most part when it comes to study a certain case of transgression. Contemporary analyses begin with the personal and end up with the social, for sin cannot be individualized. Sin is cultural. Nibbling around the edges of this serious issue from different per-spectives and schools of thought will certainly uncover a link between guilt and the moral establishment, be it religious or otherwise. If there is no link between them, then guilt is a mere fabrication, a meaningless and hollow term. Within this context, Wilfred M. McClay (2011) wonders "if we can be guilty of anything when we're accountable for nothing."[3]

Ethically, the ends are in no way separable from the means. If the means starts with an evil suggestion, the action carried out is no less evil. St. Augustine's view of sin goes even further than the inseparability between means and ends. His view, which dates back to the 5th century A.D. has been effective up to this moment. It appears in his "Commentary on the Lord's Sermon on the Mount". Committing a sin, he argues, is not dependent on whether the contemplated action is carried out. It is the intention rather than the action itself, or its con-sequences, that is sinful.[4]

In philosophy, Friedrich Nietzsche views guilt and 'bad conscience' as a kind of illness. In *The Genealogy of Morals* (1887/trans. 1989), he argues that "when faced with social norms condemning cruelty against others, a civilized human redirects his aggression towards himself".[5] Stephen Greenblatt (2005) argues that Nietzsche's view of guilt provides a useful theoretical context for understanding "the relationship between guilt and utopia".[6] This sort of aggressiveness directed inwardly is what Sigmund Freud rightly calls the sense of guilt, which has been widely implied in drama and narrative art where the motives and behavior of

---

3 W. M. McClay, *The Strange Persistence of Guilt*, in THE HEDGEHOG REVIEW, Spring 2017/19, 1, p. 23.

4 *Routledge Encyclopedia on Philosophy*, version 1.0: 2002, London, Routledge, p. 912.

5 F. Nietzsche, *The Genealogy of Morals*, 2016, available at: www.gutenberg.org/ebooks/52319, p. 300.

6 S. Greenblatt, *Will in the World*, 2005, available at: www.norton & co, p. 77.

problematic characters can be better understood by literary critics who employ this Freudian term as an approach to study complex characters.

In literature, which this study is mostly concerned with, the concept of sin and guilt takes a number of shades of feelings. It all depends on the sinner and the context of situation in which the sinful act takes place. However, guilt is uncanny in the way it appears, and it is also unique in the way it can cause pain and exert pressure on one's emotional well-being. Its negative effect can be fatal as is the case in each of Shakespeare's great tragedies, namely Hamlet, Macbeth, King Lear and Julius Caesar. It can also be less fatal but more exacting on the perpetrator who for quite a time feels totally paralyzed and unable to act. In short, the guilty person is imprisoned, at times physically, more often mentally, by his own unsettled feelings. In *The Rime of the Ancient Mariner*, Samuel Taylor Coleridge (1788) expresses this enigmatic feeling of the Mariner so skillfully.

> Since then, at an uncertain hour,
> That agony returns;
> And till my ghastly tale is told,
> This heart within me burns.[7]

Furthermore, if sin is universal in that it tempts and provokes human basic instincts, it is also contextual in that it reflects the space, time and culture in which it may thrive. In this sense, the historical and literary context of narrative art from the Seventeenth Century (the Age of Enlightenment in Europe) to date, would reflect man's telling tales about his relation to the concept of sin in a changing world. This reflection would for the most part be handled by writers of realistic fiction during that period. Apart from the allegorical significance of the story of *Robinson Crusoe* (1719) which amplifies the colonial project of the White man and his power to transform overseas nature and teach non-Whites, Daniel Defoe also dramatizes the issue of sin in *Moll Flanders* (1722) which reflects the Puritan rigid belief system and moral code, not only in England but also in the newly colonized territory called New England. Other novelists would also respond to the shifting perceptions of the world around them, both in Europe and overseas. In Nathaniel Hawthorne's *The Scarlet Letter*[8], different types of sin are represented. One of those sins is committed by Hester Prynne, who has been taken in adultery and punished by a public stigma. Her co-sinner, whose sin remains hidden, is the young church minister, Arthur Dimmesdale, who suffers for seven years but confesses to his sin while on the scaffold. The setting in which this act of sin takes place is Boston during the Puritan era. If sin is viewed as a violation of the rigid moral code of conduct, guilt is the responsibility held for the

---

7 S. T. Coleridge, "The Rime of the Ancient Mariner", in Rewey Inglis/Donald Stauffer (eds.): *Adventures in English Literature,* New York, Harcourt, Brace, 1952, p. 380.
8 N. Hawthorne, *The Scarlet Letter,* Boston, Ticknor & Fields, 1850.

violation already committed. However, at the end of the novel, there is enough room for character regeneration. Unlike the weak Arthur who could not keep his sin hidden long from the public and eventually collapses, Hester admits her sin and accepts punishment, but she learns from her sin and eventually transforms into a public figure admired for both bravery and sincerity.

For sin to be viewed as universal, I refer here to two great modern novels, one of which is *Lord of the Flies*, the other *Heart of Darkness*. The latter dramatizes the subject of sin and guilt which this paper studies in depth. In both novels, the civilized European White man finds himself away from culture and in the heart of nature to which he responds by gradually unleashing his dark instincts. In *Lord of the Flies* (1954) by William Golding, the plane carrying a bunch of British school boys crashes over an unpopulated paradise-like island in the Pacific Ocean. The children – all pre-adolescent – find themselves stranded on a tropical island with no adults, for the pilot of the plane is found dead after some time. Failing to erect an English life-style on the island, the boys divide, degenerate into tribal life and begin a merciless fight over leadership. If the concept of sin in this novel is replaced with evil, it is so because all the boys (except for the lonely Simon) try to blame their tough and bloody situation on outside forces including the "Devil": "Simon's view declares that blaming bad men, and the Devil, is both right and wrong, [...] there is evil, but it is not either outside man or confined to certain men, it is in everyone".[9]

A Freudian approach to *Lord of the Flies* as well as *Heart of Darkness* would possibly relay a clearer message about sin and guilt through the study of the concept of the sense of guilt which keeps disturbing the psyche of the two protagonists featuring in the two tales. A Freudian reading of the sense of guilt as dramatized in *Heart of Darkness* relays Conrad's message about the culpability of the civilized man when exposed to the temptations of his unleashed blind instincts in the jungle, any jungle.

A Freudian approach to sin and guilt

The literature reviewed concerning sin and guilt is quite significant for this study. However, this article chooses to focus on the concept of sense of guilt as defined and exemplified by Sigmund Freud. Freud's perception of this concept in human conduct would hopefully guide this study which seeks to unearth the motives behind an assumingly civilized person doing evil and then suffering the consequences. In his universally acclaimed book, *Civilization and Its Discontents* (1930), Sigmund Freud challenges reason as the sole prompter of human action.

---

9 W. Golding, *Lord of the Flies*, London, Noble & Barnes, 1954, p. 45.

He postulates that it is the balance among the three forces constituting our human psyche that determines how we behave and act according to the scale of values which our community has developed over time. The three forces operating within the human psyche are the *id*, the *ego* and the *superego*.[10] As theorized by Freud, the *id* is the seat of human instincts and the depot of all physical desires, including sexual satisfaction and aggressive inclinations. It functions in accordance with the pleasure principle. However, in civilization the *id* is restrained by the active *ego* which operates in line with the specifications and dictates of the socio-cultural traditions and the moral code of conduct peculiar to the community in which the constituents of the normal psyche function: "Civilization obtains mastery over the individual's dangerous desire for aggression by weakening and disarming it and by setting up an agency [the ego] within him to watch over it [...]".[11]

As administrator, the *ego* keeps trying to modify the primal urges of the *id* by adjusting its needs to the real world. In short, the *ego* mediates between potentially destructive desires and socio-moral necessities. Only in situations where the *ego* subsides, turns inactive or dormant, does the *id* erupt noisily seeking satisfaction in any way possible, not excluding homicide. The third force of the human psyche is the *superego*. It is the moral monitor commonly called 'the conscience', whose function it is to watch over human behavior according to precepts and principles inculcated by external authority, such as the state and other establishments like educational institutions. The *superego* does not directly punish the *id*. There is no traffic between the *superego* and the *id* as Freud explains. In case the *id* is provoked, it erupts to satisfy the blind basic instincts. If the *ego* fails to keep it in check, then the *superego* interferes to punish the *ego*, thus causing a sense of guilt.[12]

Arguing as such, Freud is actually questioning the very nature of human morality. He describes benevolent action and altruistic conduct as mere masks for self-gratification. Away from civilization, however, man's moral efficacy is held in check. He soon sinks back to his elemental nature and gives way to his blind instincts that seek pleasure and satisfaction through any means including all sorts of aggression. Hence the double role of man in and away from civilization. Only under insistent pangs of conscience, termed by Freud as the sense of guilt, could man manage to restore his moral capacity as a member of a civilized community.

This Freudian hypothesis explains how the constituents of the human psyche

---

10 See S. Freud, *Civilization and Its Discontents,* James Strachey (trans.), London, Norton, 1930/ trans., 1961.

11 Ivi, p. 84.

12 Ibidem.

function under or away from the eyes of Western civilization. In this regard, a study of the sense of guilt related to the two main characters, Marlow and Kurtz, who feature in Conrad's *Heart of Darkness*, would benefit much from the Freudian analysis of the human psyche. In fact, Freud's hypothesis is also supported by both Nietzsche who calls the sense of guilt "a debt unpaid yet"[13] and McClay who describes it as "the very core of [our] moral responsibility."[14] Freud even goes further when he considers the sinful deed and the intention to sin or cover up for the sinner equally guilty. Why is the intention regarded by Freud as equal to the deed? Freud answers: "[...] even when a person has not actually done the 'bad thing' but has only recognized in himself an intention to do it, he may regard himself as guilty".[15]

A Freudian analysis of sin and guilt in *Heart of Darkness*

A)   The double journey

Heart of Darkness is a literary product of the European colonial experience in Africa. It is structured along a round trip where departure and return create the pattern and rhythm of the narrative. At face value, the tale takes a European maritime mission from River Thames in England across the Atlantic Ocean to River Congo up into the African jungle. Among other crew members of the yacht *The Nellie*, Marlow, the internal narrator, is entrusted by his company to inquire about his fellow Kurtz, the ivory chief agent who for unknown reasons has stopped sending that raw material back home. However, as Marlow's African experience prompts him to insist on the 'unreality' of the whole mission, the tale assumes another turn: a journey within Marlow himself and an inquiry into "how strong the hold of civilization is on its members."[16] The three stations Marlow stops at while navigating up River Congo to check Kurtz out gradually parallel other three stations within Marlow when the conscious and unconscious forces keep acting upon his psyche in various situations.[17] In fact, as the reader sails with Marlow up River Congo in the direction of the dark jungle, he as well sails down with him in the direction of the unconscious, the *id*. The journey within parallels the journey without; their point of culmination is the stark

---

13 F. Nietzsche 1887/trans. 1989, cit., p. 22.

14 W. M. McClay, cit.

15 S. Freud 1930/trans. 1961, cit., p. 84.

16 J. Berthoud, *Joseph Conrad: The Major Phase,* Cambridge, Cambridge University Press, 1979, p. 45.

17 S. Freud 1930/trans. 1961, cit.

darkness in which all principles go inactive and man is only left with his inborn powers, if any at all, to restrain himself from committing sin.

B)   The double voice

Heart of Darkness is essentially a statement of confession that condemns the atrocities of the European Colonial period against the Black African natives and the systematic looting of their natural wealth and resources. Kurtz perishes and disappears from the scene when he is no more able to sustain himself in voluntary exile. He has allowed the dark forces of the African jungle to transform him into a monster, thus sacrificing all the cultural values that bind him to his White European civilization. Marlow, on the other hand, seems to have insisted on saving the face of Kurtz through a big lie. However, Marlow does this not through the transparency that a priestly presence entails but through loud thinking; that is, by means of evasiveness adorned by an overuse of thick irony and an atmosphere of uneasiness. Marlow admits that he does this in the hope that he might contribute to the rescue of both Kurtz's reputation as a "remarkable person"[18] and the remnants of the European civilization which in heyday has created the likes of Kurtz and sent them on unguaranteed missions to Africa and elsewhere.

Marlow tries to evade his nightmarish, jungle experience as embodied in the physically and morally degenerate Kurtz. He would dismiss the reality of that experience altogether. In fact, Marlow, for whom Kurtz has always been the dream of his life while in Europe, tries to escape the trial of the jungle where a civilized man is tested for ability to sublimate his basic instincts and primitive energies. In the jungle, instincts can be easily provoked in the darkness of the African jungle and in the absence of a check constantly exercised by civilization upon the individual psyche of its adherents.[19] Dismissing his jungle experience as notorious and unreal, Marlow is seemingly trying to survive tragic knowledge without admitting self-deception. A civilized man must resist the temptation of the jungle, as he implies. By doing this, Marlow is trying to take the crux of the experience away from its colonial context. It seems to be an act of amelioration voiced by Marlow in the nick of time to save his own face, although his last words clearly betray signs of embarrassment and discomfiture when he and Kurtz are interlocked in the jungle as double.

---

18 Ivi, p. 107.
19 Ibidem.

The voice was gone. What else had been there? But I am of course aware that next day the pilgrims buried something [Kurtz] in a muddy hole. And then they very nearly buried me.[20]

C)   Other voices from the tale

In the last scene, the two main characters, Marlow and Kurtz, voice themselves in different ways to tell the same truth about the moral impasse of the White man in the African jungle. Their voices, whether heard or unheard, resonate with overtones and undertones through which Conrad tries to describe the inward moral dilemma visited unevenly upon the inexperienced Marlow who feels guilty without ever committing a bad thing in Africa. The tale also allows passage to a number of voices, some of which remain ironically silenced. In *Heart of Darkness*, the voices of other White men encountered in the company of Marlow or at the three stations up River Congo, also contribute to the wider scope of meaning despite the low profile they keep. At the coastal station, while Marlow is questioning the absurd shelling of the African continent by the French cruiser, only the accountant, who keeps a well-organized business ledger, proves that he is part of the calculating Europe. The Manager at the Central station will not accompany Marlow any further up River Congo in search of Kurtz, because for him Kurtz does not exist anymore. The jungle has transformed him into a beast when his *id* is unleashed so freely. In the jungle, the *super ego* and the *ego* do not function as restrictive forces, for they are only the byproduct of civilization. The Manager says it flatly: "We have done all we could for him, haven't we? But there is no disguising the fact, Mr. Kurtz has done more harm than good to the Company".[21]

However, the silent voices of the faceless, black African inhabitants who fill the physical space in the Congo remain outside the context of a possible encounter or confrontation with the new invader coming from the North. The Blacks are described as beastly and savage or nude mistresses and obedient servants; they have no voices; their sick even retreat back into the jungle to die there in silence. It is only Marlow's condescension and human dignity that can see them as fellow humans, for Kurtz has already transformed them into pagans who should worship him as their own almighty 'demigod'. The polyphonic nature of the narrative as orchestrated by Conrad is meant to reflect the darkness of the colonial heart in Africa and other notorious acts related to colonization in the context of the master-slave dynamic based on power relations.

---

20 J. Conrad, cit., p. 100.
21 Ivi, p. 56.

The last scene

The last scene of *Heart of Darkness* says it all. The following excerpt from the closing pages of *Heart of Darkness* is a dialogue between Marlow and the "Intended". It is loaded with indications pointing to Marlow as Kurt's accomplice and secret sharer in genocide and ivory theft. It is quite suggestive when it comes to the dynamic of the double in terms of the Freudian understanding of the forces shaping human psyche.

> – "Forgive me. I – I – have mourned so long in silence – in silence …
> You were with him – to the last? I think of his loneliness. Nobody near to understand him as I would have understood. Perhaps no one to hear…"
> – "To the very end," I stopped in fright.
> – "Repeat them," she murmured in a heart-broken tone.
> – "I want – I want – something – something – to – to live with."
> – I was on the point of crying at her, "Don't you hear them?" The dusk was repeating them in a persistent whisper […]. *"The horror! The horror!"*
> – "His last word – to live with," she insisted. "Don't you understand I loved him – loved him – loved him!" I pulled myself together and spoke slowly.
> – "The last word he pronounced was – *your name.*"[22] (Italics mine).

Being the only eye witness to testify to the last words hardly uttered by the dying Kurtz, Marlow decides to leave the African jungle and run for his life. He flees back home to end up the myth of Kurtz with a lie. Rarely can an ordinary reader escape the weight of the ironical tone through which Marlow, playing the double here, hides the truth and speaks well of Kurtz in the presence of the Intended, Kurtz's fiancée. As a matter of fact, when Marlow and Kurtz meet for the first and last time in the latter's dark cabin, Marlow's reflection on what he has seen here is quite piercing. This is not the Kurtz he has been expecting to meet.

> I saw on that ivory face the expression of somber pride, of ruthless power, of craven terror, of an intense and hopeless despair […]. He cried in a whisper at some image, at some vision – he cried out twice, a cry that was no more than a breath: 'The Horror! The Horror!'[23]

Kurtz, here, is admitting sin and making a confession. His confession, however, is a cynical echo of that confession made by the legendary Medieval tragic hero, Faust.[24] Like Faust, who has sold his soul to the devil but is rewarded and sent to heaven after repentance, Kurtz hopes for deliverance. Yet unlike Faust, Kurtz's confession before Marlow, not before a priest, is meant to carry a universal

---

22 Ivi, p. 110.
23 Ivi, p. 100.
24 Reference is made to the tragedy of the Medieval German legendary hero featuring in *Faust*, a two-volume tragedy authored by Johann Wolfgang Goethe in 1808/trans. 1832.

message through Marlow: save the human race. There is no booming voice in the cabin, nor is there any rhetorical eloquence, just a transient vision in candle-light and a barely heard cry. It is a fair judgment passed by Kurtz on himself as well as other representatives of Europe and probably beyond that. Only here does Marlow gain full insight into the reality of Kurtz and into himself at the same time. The identification which takes place between the two men in Kurtz's dark cabin is almost complete, and the place around them has become too dark. However, Marlow's knowledge of the sin committed by Kurtz in the African jungle does not seem to absolve him from the feeling that he is Kurtz's secret sharer and partner in crime. Thus, he must say something to rid himself of the unbearable burden caused by his sense of guilt. He must play the straw man and cover up for Kurtz. In Freudian terms, Marlow's state of mind is assumingly closer to a pathological case study, for the shadow of Kurtz is still at his heels, haunting him as an obsession: "I laid the ghost of his [Kurtz's] gifts with a lie. [...] But I couldn't. I could not tell her [the truth]. It would have been too dark – too dark altogether [...]".[25]

Nonetheless, *Heart of Darkness* does register an artistic triumph on two levels associated with the issue of sin and the sense of guilt that ensues thereof. Through the heightening of the sense of guilt as experienced by both Kurtz and Marlow, a Freudian reading of this issue shows that each one of them sets his own record. Confronting the abyss, Kurtz confesses to his sin just in time, that is just moments before he passes away, to send a message about the horror facing the White man. He has not only achieved self-knowledge but also made that knowledge relevant to mankind. If Kurtz were considered a 'moral agent', the following lines would make that assumption probable, for Kurtz and Marlow end up by perceiving the same thing, although their modes of perception are not the same: "What Kurtz in the end discovers for himself is that the heart of the European citizen, for all the endeavors of his education, remains an abode of darkness, and that this truth is a terrible one".[26]

Marlow, however, recaptures our attention as the story is closing. He only succeeds to paint the bitter truth with a rosy lie to uplift the spirits of the woman in mourning, Kurtz's fiancée. As an internal narrator, Marlow has always insisted on the dreamlike form of his story. Hence the lie for a fresh start, perhaps! Marlow needs to push the trauma of his African experience into oblivion, as Albert Guerard has put it: "Only in the atonement of his lie to Kurtz's "Intended," back in the sepulchral city [in Europe], does the experience come truly to an end".[27]

The most significant point about Marlow's tale is that he chooses to tell it. In

25 Ivi, p. 111.
26 J. Berthoud, cit., p. 60.
27 A. J. Guerard, *Conrad the Novelist,* Boston, Harvard University Press, 1958, p. 88.

fact, he accepts the heavy burden and tough responsibility of trying to tolerate saying the intolerable: "To remain silent would have worsened Marlow's case of feeling guilty about his sharer in the Congo".[28]

Conclusion

Sin and the sense of guilt ensuing thereof has always been and will always be a controversial human issue. It all depends on how it is being approached. Religion – be it monotheistic or polytheistic – philosophy, ethics, psychology and other schools of thought would see sin as immoral, abhorrent and punishable. Texts to that effect are abundant across various cultures. However, literature, especially narrative art, would dramatize the issue of sin against a given socio-cultural background which frames the story being told and assigns different life functions and roles to the people featuring in that story as characters. Realistic fiction, of which Joseph Conrad's novel *Heart of Darkness* is chosen for an academic study in this article, seems to reflect life and say something significant about it. This article uses the Freudian approach to the issue of sin and the subsequent sense of guilt as dramatized in the novel through the study of two White European characters, Marlow and Kurtz. The study shows that the two main characters, under pangs of conscience and in a state of sense of guilt, turn out to be secret sharers in crime against the black Africans in the Congolese jungle. Kurtz admits his guilt while dying, while Marlow crumbles from within while telling a lie about Kurtz.

---

28 H. Laskovsky, *Blurring Images in Heart of Darkness*, in G. Deyan, *A World of Lies in Heart of Darkness*, "Journal of Language Teaching and Research", Vol. 2, N. 4, pp. 763–768, July 2011, p. 105.

Renu Josan

Contours of Morality: A Critical Study of Nathaniel Hawthorne's *The Scarlet Letter*

Introduction

Hawthorne, one of the renowned nineteenth century American novelists dealt with the theme of sin, guilt and morality in almost all his works. He belonged to the nineteenth century America where Puritanism held its sway over the society, and he himself was of the Puritan descent as he traces his ancestry to William Hathorne who had emigrated to New England from England in 1630. "He was likewise a bitter persecutor, as witness the Quakers, who had remembered him in their histories and relate an incident of his hard severity towards a woman of their sect."[1] William Hathorne's son, John Hathorne also "inherited the persecuting spirit and made himself so conspicuous in the Martyrdom of the witches, that their blood may fairly be said to have left a stain upon him."[2] Having inherited the moral earnestness of the Puritan tradition, Hawthorne was deeply concerned with the question of morality. However, Hawthorne had strong affinity with the transcendentalists who being strong advocates of democracy emphasized upon the relationship between an individual and society.

Though Emerson, the exponent of Transcendental Movement believed in the innate goodness of man, Hawthorne was concerned with the question of evil inherent in man. Hawthorne showed a streak of Puritanic gloom "deriving its strength from the Calvinistic sense of Innate Depravity and Original Sin [...] and no writer has ever wielded this terrific thought with greater terror than this same Hawthorne."[3] He studied life very minutely focusing on the hidden recesses of evil, guilt, and sin. So, it is no wonder that all his works ranging from short stories to novels are suffused with the theme of morality, *The Scarlet Letter* exemplifying it the most vividly. The origin of the novel is to be discerned in Hawthorne's notebook entries primarily dealing with the question of sin and morality. That

---

1 N. Hawthorne, *The Scarlet Letter,* Hertfordshire, Wordsworth Editions Limited, 1999, pp. 7–8.
2 Ibidem.
3 F. O. Mathiessen, *American Renaissance*, Delhi, OUP, 1973, p. 191.

the moral purpose is embedded into the novel is brought into focus in the opening chapter where the narrator commenting on the wild rosebush growing by the prison door, says:

> Finding it so directly on the threshold of our narrative, which is now about to issue from that inauspicious portal, we could hardly do otherwise than pluck one of its flowers and present it to the reader. It may serve, let us hope, to symbolize some sweet moral, blossom that may be found along the track or relief, the darkening close of a tale of human frailty and sorrow.[4]

But before venturing into an analysis of *The Scarlet Letter* from a moral perspective, it is befitting to know about morality, ethics, and its various dimensions.

What is morality

The word 'morality,' derived from the Latin word, *moralitas* meaning manner, character or proper behaviour, refers to the categorization of one's intentions, desires, and actions as proper or improper. Morals may refer to a set of principles derived from a code of conduct followed by a particular religion or culture or they may be based on an individual's beliefs which he believes to be universal. Different systems of expressing morality have been formulated, like ontological-ethical systems which adhere to a set of established rules and normative ethical systems which are based on the merit of the actions. Moral behaviour does not constitute simply the virtues of honesty, impartiality, but also incorporates motives and intentions. It is imperative to gain knowledge of the feelings of others and it is the affective domain which becomes more significant than mere cognitive approach. Though emotions and reason have always been conflicting poles in the domain of morality, a balance has to be struck between the two. Carol Gilligan, a famous American psychologist, attributes care dimension to morality in that the uniqueness of people, situations, and relationships take central position. Durkheim regards morality as a meaningful concept only in the context of society that serves as the ground for individual growth and development. German philosopher Kant defined morality in terms of 'heteronomy' and 'autonomy of will.' Drawing upon Kant and Durkheim, Piaget elaborates on the concept of conventional morality and rational morality, where in, when the conduct depends on approach of others, it is guided by the heteronomy of will or conventional morality, and when the individual reaches a stage of autonomy of will, his behaviour is directed by his/her own rational and moral choices or rational

---

4 H. Claridge, "Introduction", *The Scarlet Letter*, cit., p. ix.

morality. Keeping in view the different aspects entailed in the concept of morality, a careful analysis of the contours of morality as portrayed in *The Scarlet Letter* will be attempted.

Outline and setting of the novel

The novel is basically a tale of adultery committed by Hester Prynne and Dimmesdale, the pastor, for which Hester is imprisoned and when released, is made to stand on the scaffold in full public view, wearing letter 'A' on her chest. The story takes a dramatic turn with the arrival of Chillingworth, the estranged husband who is keen to find out the person with whom Hester had illicit relationship. The novel simply does not delineate the adulterous relationship, rather it dwells intensely on the consequences of sin, therein presenting a deep psychological analysis, and also confronting the reader with the question of what constitutes moral or immoral behaviour. In order to resolve the debate regarding Hester being an angel or an adulteress, it is necessary to analyse the conditions in the mid-nineteenth century when the novel was written, and the seventeenth century Boston which serves as the setting of the novel. The introductory chapter to novel describes the society at length in which Hester Prynne is to be tried for adultery. Hawthorne describes the place being suffused with the "chilliest of social atmosphere."[5]

Elaborating on the setting of the novel, Kathryn VanSpanckeren opines, "*The Scarlet Letter* which is set in Boston around 1650 during early Puritan Colonization emphasizes the Calvinistic obsession towards morality, sexual repression, shame and declaration of guilt and spiritual salvation."[6] The people who had come to witness the punishment meted out to Hester Prynne for her adulterous action had "the same solemnity of demeanour […] as befitted a people among whom religion and law were identical."[7] Religion and law were so deeply ingrained in their personalities that "the mildest and severest acts of public discipline were alike made venerable and awful."[8] The novelist makes it clear that one could not expect any sympathy "that a transgressor might look for, from such bystanders."[9]

When Hester comes out from the prison along with her child Pearl, she is made to stand on the scaffold, wearing letter 'A' on her chest. The sight of Hester

---

5　*The Scarlet Letter*, cit., p. 9.
6　K. VanSpanckeren, *Outline of American Literature (M)*, USA, The US Information Agency, 1994, p. 37.
7　*The Scarlet Letter*, cit., p. 37.
8　Ibidem.
9　Ibidem.

holding her baby in her arms did not evoke any kind of sympathy for the victim. Instead, she was subjected to derision and humiliation with one of the women gathered there saying, "This woman has brought shame upon us all and ought to die. Is there no law for it!"[10] These women feel that a much more severe punishment should have been meted out to Hester than what has been given by the magistrate. Says one, "If the hussy stood up for judgement before us five that are now here in knot together, would she come off with a sentence as the worshipful magistrates have awarded?"[11]

Chillingworth, Hester's estranged husband could have accepted her and released her from the ignominy and humiliation that she suffered but he chooses not to do so. Commenting on Chillingworth's act, Hawthorne says, "the man whose connection with the fallen woman had been the most intimate and sacred of them all [decides] not to be pilloried beside her on her pedestal of shame."[12] The novel cannot be read simply as either condoning the two lovers or accusing them instead the novel compels the reader towards the recognition that it is not a matter of one view or the other, rather it involves the analysis, a careful probing of the web of complex relationships interfused with the ubiquitous question of morality.

Hester standing on the scaffold in undoubtedly guilty but the question arises: Is she solely responsible for the act? Does she deserve such a punishment? Has she deliberately transgressed the moral law instituted by the Puritan magistrates who assumed self-righteous importance? In order to seek answers to these questions, Hester's relationship with Chillingworth, and Dimmesdale needs to be analysed. Viewed from the perspective of Puritan society, Hester has transgressed the moral laws. But the novelist raises a question, "Has Hester sinned alone?"[13] Elaborating on this aspect, he says further, "if the outward guise of purity is but a lie, and that, if truth were everywhere to be shown, a scarlet letter would blaze forth on many a bosom besides Hester Prynne."[14] Moreover, Hawthorne appears to be critical of the "sacredness of the divine institutions"[15] possessed by the Puritan theocracy in the novel, and he seems to be questioning the ability of the Puritan magistrates to pass a fair judgement on Hester as though they invest themselves with the moral authority of God, they lack the "power to sympathise?"[16]

---

10 Ivi, p. 39.

11 Ivi, p. 38.

12 R. H. Millington (ed.), *The Cambridge Companion to Nathaniel Hawthorne*, Cambridge, CUP, 2004, p. 173.

13 *The Scarlet Letter*, cit., p. 65.

14 Ibidem.

15 R. H. Millington, cit., p. 165.

16 Ibidem.

Hester's sin is revealed to the public in the form of her daughter Pearl, the result of her secret liaison with Dimmesdale but Dimmesdale's sin remains locked in his heart. The identity of Chillingworth as Hester's husband remains hidden, and he is known to the people as an expert in medicine. So, he manages to keep himself out of the ambit of Puritan morality. However, Chillingworth's guilt becomes apparent when he makes his appearance in the Scaffold scene and in his subsequent actions. The novel portrays different types of sin as the sins of the flesh, sins of weakness, sins of will and the intellect exhibited by the different characters. Now, the pertinent and prominent aspect of morality will be examined separately for each of the main characters, thereby defining the contours of morality.

Chillingworth

When Chillingworth meets Hester in the jail, after being away for so many years, the private discussion does not reflect any kind of harmony or warmth of feelings. Instead he makes a confession that he had made a mistake in marrying Hester. He admits "I – man of thought [...] a man already in decay, having given my best years to feed the hungry dream of knowledge – what had I to do with youth and beauty like thine own?"[17] In a similar vein, Hester makes a candid statement, "Thou knowest that I was frank with thee. I felt no love, nor feigned any."[18] This conversation makes it clear that the conjugal relationship between Hester and Chillingworth was not based on love, harmony, intimacy, and mutual consideration which are so integral to a harmonious and stable relationship. Selfishness had led Chillingworth to marry Hester a young, beautiful, and passionate girl. He realizes that they have wronged each other but he states clearly that his was the first wrong, "when I betrayed thy budding youth into a false and unnatural relation with my decay."[19] Chillingworth's wrong cannot be condoned as knowing full well about his physical deformity and deep inclination towards attaining knowledge, he had lured Hester into an illusory trap of forming a fruitful and harmonious alliance. He has committed a 'fouler offence' in that he had persuaded her to fancy herself happy by his side, "when her heart knew no better."[20]

Moreover, goaded by an intense desire to find out the person involved in the adulterous relationship with Hester, Chillingworth puts in his best endeavours to

---

17 *The Scarlet Letter*, cit., p. 55.
18 Ivi, p. 56.
19 Ibidem.
20 Ivi, p. 132.

find out the identity of that person. Commenting on his endeavour, Hawthorne says, "Few secrets can escape an investigator who has opportunity and license to undertake such a quest and skill to follow it up."[21] Chillingworth grows suspicious about Dimmesdale being the person engaged in adulterous relationship and seeks an opportunity to live with Dimmesdale, the pastor on the pretext of curing the pastor as he possessed a sound knowledge of medicine.

Despite being a scholar, Chillingworth renounces all sense of morality and is seized with a burning desire of avenging himself. His 'calm, meditative, scholarlike' appearance gave way to an ugly, evil and malicious expression. People wondered if he was 'diabolic agent' who "had the divine permission for a season to burrow into the clergyman's intimacy and plot against his soul."[22] On being confirmed about his suspicion regarding Dimmesdale, Chillingworth is overcome with a feeling of wild "wonder, joy, and horror."[23] Comparing his joy with that of Satan's, author opines, "Had a man seen old Roger Chillingworth at that moment in his ecstasy, he would have had no need to ask how Satan comports himself when a precious human soul is lost to heaven and won into his kingdom."[24] Adopting devious means to find out the identity of the wrongdoer and making Dimmesdale suffer utmost pain, anguish, and suffering, Chillingworth commits a sin worse than that of Hester and Dimmesdale. Surprisingly, the Puritan society does not consider him a sinner rather a well-wisher of Dimmesdale. Chillingworth is filled with "a depth of malice" which leads him to imagine a more intimate "revenge than any mortal had wreaked upon an enemy."[25]

Chillingworth is a sinner on two counts, first he has gone against the sacred vows of marriage, wherein he fails to fulfill the marital responsibilities, and secondly, as said by Dimmesdale, "He has violated in cold blood, the sanctity of human heart."[26] According to Hawthorne, this is a grave sin which is exhibited by Chillingworth as he committed, "the sin of an intellect, that triumphed over the sense of brotherhood with man and reverence for God."[27] Burning with a keen desire to destroy the soul of Dimmesdale by exposing him in front of the public, he clings to Dimmesdale like a leech, and under the pretence of curing Dimmesdale's ailment and sympathizing with his anguish, he derives malignant pleasure. However, Chillingworth's plan stands thwarted as Dimmesdale in his final address to the public confesses his wrong doing but this is taken by the

---

21 Ivi, p. 92.
22 Ivi, p. 95.
23 Ivi, p. 103.
24 Ibidem.
25 Ivi, p. 104.
26 Ivi, p. 146.
27 R. H. Millington, cit., p. 346.

people as an expression of extreme humility and modesty. Dimmesdale considers Chillingworth as a sinner worse than they were as he has committed sins of the will and intellect which are the worst of all the sins. Finally, the realization dawns upon Chillingworth that he has behaved in a fiendish manner in tormenting Dimmesdale but by then, his soul has become so degenerated and devoid of all grace that he only feels a kind of repugnance and meets his tragic end consumed by his own malicious and vicious nature.

Dimmesdale

Unlike Chillingworth, who falls into the deepest abyss of viciousness and sin, depriving himself of any hope of redemption, Dimmesdale, though engaged in an illicit relationship, stands redeemed. Dimmesdale undergoes worse punishment than Hester, in that he keeps the guilt confined to his heart and continues to suffer in silence for seven long years. Commenting on the ill effects of hidden guilt on the person, Ellen White writes, "Grief, anxiety, discontent, remorse guilt, distrust, all tend to break down the life forces and to invite decay and death."[28] Dimmesdale is destroyed by the concealment of the guilt, though he sincerely repents for his "thoughtless surrender to passion."[29] Like many Puritans, "he made it his custom to fast not for rendering the body fitter medium of celestial illumination but rigorously and until his knees trembled beneath him as an act of penance."[30] Quite often Dimmesdale tortured himself with a bloody scourge.

The novelist describes Dimmesdale as "a true priest, a true religionist with the reverential sentiment largely developed."[31] "Weighed down by his overpowering sense of guilt," Dimmesdale tells the congregation that "he was the worst of sinners" but he "reaches astonishing heights in the pulpit and in the affection and esteem of his parishioners."[32] In the final scene when Hester devises a plan to escape to a new place, Dimmesdale knows that for him escape is impossible and instead decides to address the congregation confessing his sin. Though in his address he admits himself to be a sinner saying, "ye that have loved me! – ye, that have me holy! – behold me here, the one sinner of the world!"[33] but the people

---

28 G. E. White, Ministry *of Healing,* Idaho, Pacific Press Association, 1942. p. 241.

29 F. Crew, *The Sin of the Fathers: Hawthorne's Psychological Themes,* London, OUP, 1996, p. 137.

30 *The Scarlet Letter,* cit., p. 108.

31 Ivi, p. 92.

32 A. Turner, *Nathaniel Hawthorne: An Introduction and Interpretation,* New York, Holt, Rineheart, and Winston, 1961, p. 59.

33 *The Scarlet Letter,* cit., p. 190.

take his confession to be "a parable, [...] that, in the view of infinite Purity, we are sinners all alike."[34]

Judged by the laws of Puritan morality, Dimmesdale has undoubtedly committed a sin but he stands condemned only mildly if at all by the writer. Though Dimmesdale is destroyed by the concealment of his violation of the moral code of conduct; he stands absolved of his sins by indulging in sincere repentance. Viewed from the perspective of Dimmesdale, the hypocrisy of the Puritan laws stands exposed in that it fails to recognize the sinner in Dimmesdale. The writer brings into focus this very aspect of society which does not take into consideration the motive, the circumstances under which sin is committed. The domain of morality has always been entangled in the conflict between reason and emotion. Ethics defines the code that a society adheres while morality probes into the depths of right and wrong at a much deeper level, both personal and spiritual. Morality may also be viewed as a combination of caring, judging, and acting. Dimmesdale may have been a sinner according to 'conventional morality,' but he cannot be considered a sinner from the perspective of 'rational morality,' wherein the person's behaviour is guided by his own rational, moral choices. Moreover, moral behaviour just does not comprise only virtues like honesty and impartiality but it also includes motives and intentions. Following indiscriminately a particular line of action in accordance with a moral code of conduct devised by the society is not the only signifier of moral actions as it invariably depends on circumstances. The affective domain is to be given equal importance as the cognitive approach as both are significant contributors in the moral development of an individual. Dimmesdale's efforts to bring about spiritual upliftment of the people, his dedication and devotion towards their welfare vouch for his focus on, "the relation between the Deity and the communities of mankind."[35]

Moreover, Dimmesdale has never gone "beyond the scope of generally received laws although, in a single instance he had so fearfully transgressed one of the most sacred of them."[36] However, Hawthorne seems to be absolving him by commenting that "this had been a sin of passion not of principle, nor even purpose,"[37] and for that he had "kept his conscience alive and painfully sensitive by the fretting of an unhealed wound,"[38] thereby making himself "safer within the line of virtue."[39] Being a human, Dimmesdale was susceptible to all the worldly passions but realizing the grave sin that he had committed, he "had

---

34 Ivi, p. 194.
35 Ivi, p. 249.
36 Ivi, p. 150.
37 Ibidem.
38 Ivi, p. 151.
39 Ibidem.

watched with morbid zeal and minuteness – each breath of emotion, and his every thought."[40] Finally, Dimmesdale succeeds in redeeming himself when at the moment of his death, he exposes himself as the sinner before the, "horror stricken multitude [...] concentrated on the ghastly miracle."[41] Dimmesdale, "stood with a flush of triumph on his face, as one who in the crisis of acutest pain had won a victory,"[42] evoking a sense of awe and wonder among the multitude.

Hester

As regards Hester, the central pivot on which the entire novel hinges, the question that looms large is whether the letter 'A' that she wears on her chest signifies her being an angel or an adulteress. This contradiction regarding Hester is made evident in the introductory chapter itself, 'The Customs House,' where the narrator comes across a few sheets describing the life of Hester Prynne, wherein, "she gained from many people the reverence due to an angel, but, I should imagine was looked upon others as an intruder or a nuisance."[43] When Hester is led out of the prison and drawn forward by the jailor, she is presented as someone imbued with the fierce spirit of individual dignity and force of character. She steps out "into the open air as if by her own free will."[44] Though charged with adultery and punished to stand on the scaffold, "fully revealed before the crowd," she "appeared more lady-like."[45] But the people who had expected to see "her dimmed and obscured by the disastrous cloud were astonished [...] to perceive how her beauty shown out and made a halo of misfortune and ignominy in which she was enveloped."[46]

Furthermore, stressing upon the perception of the people regarding Hester, termed adulteress according to the strict Puritan code of morality, Hawthorne says, a Papist, "might have seen in this beautiful woman [...] an object to remind him of the image of Divine Maternity [...] something which should remind him [...] of that sacred image of sinless motherhood."[47] Unfortunately, the society saw only "the taint of deepest sin in the most sacred quality of human life, working such effect that the world was only the darker for the woman's beauty

---

40 Ivi, p. 150.
41 Ivi, p. 191.
42 Ibidem.
43 Ivi, p. 24.
44 Ivi, p. 39.
45 Ivi, pp. 39–40.
46 Ivi, p 40.
47 Ivi, p. 42.

and the more lost for the infant."[48] Hester has certainly violated the moral code of conduct but the question arises is she to be viewed only as an adulteress without taking into consideration the noble and generous acts that she engages herself with when released from the prison.

It is necessary to probe into Hester's marital life wherein may lie the reason for her one act of transgression. Hester is made to enter into a loveless marital relationship with a man "slightly deformed with the left shoulder a trifle higher than the right."[49] Moreover, being inclined towards scholarly pursuits, he fails to fulfill the marital responsibilities in that he disappears leaving her all alone. The physical aspect of love in marriage cannot be negated and erotic passions cannot be termed as "the blackness of man's heart."[50] The novelist recognizes the importance of the "force of erotic love,"[51] and seems to be advocating better relations between men and women. Hawthorne must have been influenced by the work of Margaret Fuller, *Woman in the Nineteenth Century* (1845) where she stresses upon the interrelatedness of the public and domestic domains, and that both men and women inhabit a common world "albeit differently."[52]

Hester stands condemned according to the Puritan law which believes that an individual cannot attain salvation through righteous actions. However, Hawthorne seems to be questioning if not outrightly rejecting, the Puritan law which does not take into consideration the feelings of caring, generosity, and sympathy. Hester succeeds in redeeming herself as she decides to stay back in New England, the place of her punishment thinking that the daily insults that she would be subjected to, "would at length purge her soul, and work out another purity that which she had lost: more saint-like, because the result of martyrdom."[53] She spends her money in looking after the "wretches less miserable than herself."[54] Moreover, Hester counsels and provides solace to people with "sorrows and perplexities especially women in the continually recurring trials of wounded, wasted, wronged, misplaced or erring and sinful passion"[55] By portraying Hester as a person full of mercy and commiseration for others, Hawthorne drives home the point that the ideal Christian community should be based on charity, mercy rather than severe judgement and inflexible dogmatic rules.

Hawthorne does not simply reflect Hester's charitable qualities but goes beyond implying that her inward rebellion is imbued with heroism. Com-

---

48 Ibidem.
49 Ivi, p. 44.
50 Ivi, p. 168.
51 R. H. Millington, cit., p. 167.
52 Ivi, p. 81.
53 *The Scarlet Letter*, cit., p. 61.
54 Ivi, p. 63.
55 Ivi, pp. 196–197.

menting on this aspect, Gary Scharnhorst says, "Her personal moral strength transcends her suffering and transforms her punishment into self-designed grace."[56] Hawthorne's idea that good works do help in redeeming oneself is brought out clearly when Hester tells Dimmesdale that he has atoned for his sin and need no longer feel sinful. She exhorts, "Is there no reality in the penitence thus sealed and witness by good works? And wherefore should it not bring you peace?"[57] Hester and Dimmesdale did not violate "the sanctity of human heart,"[58] rather as Hester says the relationship "had a consecration of its own."[59] By throwing away the letter 'A' from the bosom into the forest, Hester discards her past stained with the stigma of adultery. This act of hers may not receive the approval of the Puritans but seems to have definitely received the approval of heaven as "All at once, as with a sudden smile of heaven. Forth burst the sunshine [...] gleaming adown the grey trunks of the solemn trees."[60] Nature sympathized with "the bliss of these two spirits."[61] Being true to oneself is of greater significance than the dogmas and norms of society. Hester has been true to her own self and insists on beginning 'all anew' advising Dimmesdale to "exchange this false life of thine for a true one"[62] thereby enjoying the happiness that awaits them in a new place. Thus, Hester reflects the views of Hawthorne that, "the angel and apostle of the coming revelation must be a woman, indeed, but lofty, pure and beautiful and wise, [...] and showing how sacred love should make us happy by the truest test of a life successful to such an end."[63]

Conclusion

The Puritan society with its self-righteous persecution of Hester deprives itself of the generosity and love ingrained in Hester. Francis O. Mathiessen compares the aspect of moral recognition in the novel to that of the Greek tragedies in that Hawthorne's characters become aware of the immoral deeds and thus, "participate in the purgatorial movement, the movement towards regeneration."[64] Hester and Dimmesdale succeed in achieving redemption like Shakespeare's Lear but Chillingworth falls into such deepest depths of hatred and malice that he

---

56 G. Scharnhorst, *The Critical Response to Nathaniel Hawthorne's The Scarlet Letter,* Westport, Greenwood Press, 1992, p. 224.
57 *The Scarlet Letter,* cit., p. 144.
58 Ivi, p. 146.
59 Ibidem.
60 Ivi, p. 153.
61 Ibidem.
62 Ivi, p. 148.
63 Ivi, p. 197.
64 F. O. Mathiessen, cit., p. 350.

feels subjected to a kind of self-abhorrence and repugnance and finally withers away.

The novelist does not promote judgementalism, described by John M. Fowler as "that attitude of arrogance by which one assumes an air of superiority over others by constantly indulging in criticism, fault finding and an unforgiving spirit towards others while ignoring the same faults in oneself."[65] Moreover, the novel remains open neither reflecting sympathy for the condemned lovers nor approval though the need to change the system in emphasized throughout. The novel begins with the description of the Puritans' attempt to establish a 'new world' but as the novel progresses, focus is on Hester's affirmation of the need to revamp the system which would necessitate "the whole system of society to be torn down, and built up anew"[66] and the establishment of "a whole relation between man and woman on a surer ground of mutual happiness."[67] The novelist creates a kind of dilemma in that he castigates the existing laws but at the same time does not permit violating the laws; which is clearly evident in dying Dimmesdale's answer to Hester's query if they will ever meet again. Dimmesdale says, "The law we broke! – the sin here so awfully revealed […] it was vain to hope that we could meet hereafter, in an everlasting and pure reunion."[68]

Considering the rigid Puritan environment in which Hawthorne lived, he could not have indulged in an open criticism of the laws. However, Hawthorne's sympathy for the lovers and lack of "reverence for the infallibility of superior persons,"[69] can be easily gleaned through the pages of the novel. Had the novelist not supported Hester, he would not have commented, "The Scarlet Letter had not done its office."[70]

In his approach towards tackling the problem of evil inherent in human beings, the novelist seems to be echoing words of Isabella in Shakespeare's *Measure for Measure*, where in a plea is made to temper justice with mercy, and Hawthorne advocates a harmonious blend of 'conventional' and 'rational' morality. Though the question of evil looms large over the novel, yet the novelist, "was most able to affirm the warmth and strength of the heart and to create a sense not merely of life's inexorability and sordidness, but of its possibilities of beauty and grandeur."[71]

---

65 J. M. Fowler, *Should We Ever Judge Others?* "Dialogue", 11 (2 1999), 28.
66 R. H. Millington, cit., p. 164.
67 *The Scarlet Letter*, cit., p. 197.
68 Ivi, p. 256.
69 R. H. Millington, cit., p. 775.
70 *The Scarlet Letter*, cit., p. 124.
71 F. O. Mathiessen, cit., p. 351.

Eloïse Sureau-Hale

Parodies and Perversions: A Study of the Various Forms of Transgression in *Maldoror*

Introduction

Sin is alluring. A forbidden act, a forbidden relationship, forbidden fruit, what could be more tempting? What could be more enticing than to walk the edge between the acceptable and the reprehensible? What could be more satisfying than to read about a character who perpetrates all the atrocities one wishes one could perform if only morality and law were suspended? Published in 1869 by Isidore Ducasse, under the penname Count of Lautréamont,[1] *Maldoror* is one of the most perverted pieces of 19th century literature, because it challenges the accepted moral conventions of the day. Sin and transgression are not only two of the main themes of the text, they *are* the text. Ducasse suggests that so-called morality is merely social tradition devoid of any real truth. He challenges the perfection of God and condemns Him as a sinner even lower than man. In a letter to his editor Poulet-Malassis dated October 23d 1869, Ducasse made the claim that he was presenting a new form of literature, based on previous literary currents, but going further:

> I have sung of evil as did Misckiewickz, Byron, Milton, Southey, A. de Musset, Baudelaire, etc. Naturally I have somewhat exaggerated the diapason so as to do something new in the way of this sublime literature which sings of despair only to oppress the reader and make him desire the good as remedy.[2]

He succeeded in doing so by utilizing a certain number of transgressions simultaneously, something which few, if any, had done before.

A transgression is an act that goes against a law, rule, or accepted social code; an offense. This essay will study three forms of transgression. The first part will focus on transgression as manifested within the content of the text. We will begin with intertextuality and palimpsests, investigating how Ducasse exploits earlier

---

1 Lautréamont, *Les Chants de Maldoror*, Engl. Trans. *Maldoror and the Complete Works of Comte de Lautréamont*, Cambridge, Exact Change, 2011.
2 Ivi, p. 258.

novels. Of particular interest is Matthew Lewis' Gothic novel *The Monk*. Ducasse uses the transgression inherent within Lewis' text to create a new genre that is grounded in established standards like those of the Gothic novel, but further challenges the boundaries of the acceptable. We will also, through the examination of a few chosen images, analyze how and why Ducasse perverts the accepted definition of transgression itself, and upends the concept. The second part will look at translation as a transgression, examining how the process of translation perverts the original. The final part will concentrate on the techniques Ducasse uses to break narratological conventions. How does this transgression of structures pose a challenge to the act of reading, forcing the reader to involve himself or herself to a larger degree than in other texts? The essay's conclusion will define the purpose for the text as a whole. We will place *Maldoror* in modernity along with the reasons why the text is still not only read today, but studied by 21st century scholars.

Transgression of content: challenging accepted beliefs

From the very first pages, the narrator (who at times is the protagonist Maldoror and at times is not) warns the reader that unless he is capable of logical thought and mental attention, he should not cross the boundaries of such a text:

> May it please heaven that the reader, emboldened, and become momentarily as fierce as what he reads, find without loss of bearing a wild and abrupt way across the desolate swamps of these somber, poison-filled pages. [...] It would not be good for everyone to read the pages which follow; only a few may relish this bitter fruit without danger.[3]

The reader is soon introduced to Maldoror in just a few words, setting the stage:

> I shall set down in a few lines how upright Maldoror was during his early years, when he lived happy. There: done. He later perceived he was born wicked: strange mischance! For a great many years he concealed his character as best he could; but in the end, because his effort was not natural to him, each day the blood would rush to his head until, unable any longer to bear such a life, he hurled himself resolutely into a career of evil [...] sweet atmosphere![4]

Maldoror's fall is a conflation of both the Fall of Lucifer from Heaven and the Fall of Man in the Garden of Eden. From then on, the narration will reveal scenes of atrocity, at times difficult to bear, from rape to disembowelment to cold-blooded murder.

Ducasse turns the definition of transgression on its ear. What we typically see

---

3 Ivi, p. 27.
4 Ivi, p. 29.

as a transgression he praises as a good deed. What we see as a laudable action, he condemns as a transgression. In his *Poésies* published after *Maldoror* and under his real name, Ducasse develops a sort of writing manifesto, listing the writers that have influenced his own textual production, if only to label them the "Great-Soft-Heads of our epoch".[5] One of his most famous claims is to state that "Poetry must be made by all. Not by one".[6] By praising plagiarism and reversal, Ducasse allows the reader a glimpse of his list of writers. Through this list and the darkness inherent to the narration, it becomes apparent that *Maldoror* draws from Gothic literature. There is a twist, however: *Maldoror* pushes the boundaries, taking the reader to the edge of the acceptable, giving birth to what Edmund Burke[7] could have labeled "Sublime Plus"; more sublime than Sublime itself. There is within the text a deliberate will to disturb:

> Lautréamont forces his readers to stop taking their world for granted. He shatters the complacent acceptance of the reality proposed by their cultural traditions, and makes them see that reality for what it is: an unreal nightmare all the more hair-raising because the sleeper believes that he is awake.[8]

Even though Isidore Ducasse lists in *Poésies* numerous Gothic authors, whose contribution to the creation of *Maldoror* one recognizes in reading the cantos, this study will choose to focus on *The Monk*[9] as *Maldoror*'s main subtext, and will analyze briefly how Ducasse parodied Matthew Lewis' creation, as Lewis himself exaggerated the Gothic trends that had come before him. As Ducasse clearly states in *Poésies:* "Plagiarism is necessary. Progress implies it".[10]

In "The 1790s: the effulgence of Gothic" Robert Miles describes Lewis' *The Monk* as follows:

> *The Monk* is the most extraordinary owing to its desire to represent everything that had gone before in transgressive excess. In Lewis' novel, everything was the same and yet everything was different.[11]

> [...] *The Monk* was shockingly new, because it inverted, parodied, or exaggerated the features it cannibalized.[12]

---

5 Ivi, p. 232.

6 Ivi, p. 244.

7 See E. Burke, *A Philosophical Enquiry in to the Origins of our Ideas of the Sublime and Beautiful*, Oxford, Oxford University Press, 1990.

8 A. De Jonge, *Nightmare Culture. Lautréamont and Les Chants de Maldoror*, New York, St Martin's Press, 1973, p. 1.

9 M. Lewis, *The Monk*, London, Penguin, 1998.

10 Lautréamont, *Maldoror*, cit., p. 240.

11 R. Miles, *The 1790s: the effulgence of Gothic in The Cambridge Companion to Gothic Fiction*, Cambridge, Cambridge University Press, 2002, p. 52.

12 Ivi, p. 53.

In *The Monk*, every feature of the Gothic novel is depicted: labyrinths and dark passages under convents and abbeys; deviance, darkness, vengeance, murder, corruption, ghosts, devil-worshipping, to name just a few. As Robert Miles notes, *The Monk* represents an exaggeration. Ambrosio's sexual appetite for instance is almost supernatural in its intensity. A strong feeling of dread and shock arises from the situations described. Lewis utilized the Gothic works that had come before him, but brazenly pushed the limits of the genre, placing his characters in scandalous circumstances. Once Ambrosio discovers the pleasures of the flesh, thanks to Matilda's ploy to infringe on the monks' regulations and enter the monastery disguised as a young novice, his appetite knows no bounds. Later on, in order to possess the young maiden Antonia, Ambrosio will not hesitate to murder her mother as she is about to unveil his scheme. He aims to seduce the woman's daughter Antonia, without knowing that they are his mother and sister respectively. In *The Monk*, every element of the Gothic is amplified:

> Like many other terror novelists, Lewis is less concerned with developing characters and a consistent point of view and more interested in creating arresting tableaux, or scenes that shock, something he achieves through his inversions of generic expectations. To a degree *The Monk* is a series of these scenic inversions. Spectacle, not narrative, is Lewis's motivating force.[13]

Instead of focusing on a couple of themes or elements of the Gothic, Matthew Lewis uses them all, including the presence of the supernatural in the forms of the Bleeding Nun and Satan, as well as narrations within narrations, creating various "mises en abyme" to amplify the effect.

A relationship that Gérard Genette termed "a complex transposition" exists between *Maldoror* and *The Monk,* one in which a text imitates another including mimicking the style of the original.[14] Ducasse draws his inspiration from both the style and the images presented in *The Monk*. If *The Monk* shaped a new genre in accumulating all the Gothic elements and exaggerating them, *Maldoror* uses the same model and goes further, appropriating *The Monk* and turning the situations presented there into even more ruthless acts of depravity and debauchery. Mathilda corrupts Ambrosio and leads him to a life of crime, the least of which is the breaking of his pious vows. When Ambrosio discovers the pleasures that flesh provides, however, his appetite remains in the domain of the accepted sexual conduct of the time: between a man and a woman. Maldoror, however, preys on young boys, enhancing the sexual transgression by combining both the taboos of gender (homosexuality) and age (an adult who seduces preteens). He titillates the youths and plays with their innocence, not unlike

---

13 Ivi, pp. 53–54.
14 See G. Genette, *Palimpsestes*, Paris, Seuil, 1982.

Goethe's Erl-King.[15] He entices them to take on a life of crime. Rage against mankind in general and adults in particular is a recurring theme in *Maldoror*. Cutting short the lives of young boys before they can become adults is a frequent goal of Maldoror himself, considering the narrator's hatred of all things adult. Preventing the young from growing old may be perceived as a salvation, à la Peter Pan.[16] *Maldoror* endeavors to represent mankind as the weakest link in the Great Chain of Being,[17] which is in fact reversed in the text, with insects like lice often depicted as admirable for their ability to cause mankind discomfort and pain:

> Lice are incapable of wreaking as much ill as their imaginations contemplate. If you find a louse in your way, be off, and do not lick the papillae of its tongue. You would meet with an accident. That has been known. No matter, I am already content with the amount of harm the louse does you. O human race: I only wish it could do still more.[18]

If the breaking of the Ten Commandments is praised throughout the six cantos, it is also flaunted and paraded about in the reader's face:

> Truth and freedom will only be attained through basic transgression. This is the fundamental theme of *Les Chants*. Law and taboo are barriers erected by culture to cut its victims off from the truth. Such barriers can only be broken down by saying the unsayable, thinking the unthinkable.[19]

The Monk portrays the institution of the Church and its most venerated priest Ambrosio as depraved and decadent; the people's idol, their acclaimed religious model is in fact a vile creature. *Maldoror* goes further; perhaps the most flagrant and recurrent example of transgression is the portrayal of the one the narrator calls "The Creator." Where Matthew Lewis portrayed the downfall of a high priest, Ducasse exposes the downfall of the figure of God.

At first glance, *Maldoror* can be mistakenly perceived as a simple parable of the struggle between good and evil. Many elements are inverted in the text, however, starting with the Great Chain of Being. The purpose of the chain is ordered categorization that establishes regimented distinctions. Ducasse's purpose is to create disorder. At the top of the chain, the Creator is supposed to preside over his Creation. The Creator in *Maldoror*, however, constitutes an ambiguous character, endlessly clashing with the protagonist for, presumably,

---

15 Goethe's "Der Erlkönig" is a poem published in 1782 in which a young boy is enticed by a supernatural being and eventually taken and killed.

16 In *The Rebel*, Albert Camus asserts that Ducasse's revolt is anchored in his being a teenager, rebelling at the same time against creation and against himself. A. Camus, *The Rebel: an Essay on Man in Revolt*, New York, Vintage Books, 1991.

17 For a thorough analysis of the concept of the Great Chain of Being from Plato to the 19th century, see Arthur Lovejoy's comprehensive study.

18 Lautréamont, *Maldoror*, cit., p. 80.

19 A. De Jonge, *Nightmare Culture. Lautréamont and Les Chants de Maldoror*, cit., p. 49.

domination over mankind. Interestingly, the Creator is only defined by his function, thus he is reduced to a mere manufacturer, whose progeny he shows great malice toward: "I have seen the Creator, spurring on his needless cruelty, setting alight conflagrations in which old people and children perished!"[20] Maldoror and the Creator take on numerous forms in their struggle. Each transforms into beasts and objects of all shapes and sizes in order to better annihilate the other: a task they are never able to complete. *Maldoror* represents a recognized reversal, an exchanging of conventional and established notions for acts typically defined as transgressions.

Even though the Creator's abode remains on high, his actions consistently paint him as a low figure. There are a few instances in the text in which the Creator is portrayed as depraved, thus allowing the narrator to violate the norms by sullying the one that should be worshipped. Although the text abounds in examples, two in particular are noteworthy. In the first instance, located in the second canto, the narrator raises his head to the sky. As he scans further and further, he unexpectedly chances upon the Creator:

> [...] I raised my dismayed gaze higher, still higher, until I caught sight of a throne fashioned of human excrement and gold upon which, with idiotic pride, body swathed in a shroud made of unwashed hospital sheets, sat he who calls himself the Creator.[21]

The Creator's depiction, though disgraceful, is still full of irony and humor, at least for one with a strong stomach: He is sitting in a pool of blood from which He is plucking handfuls of human beings that He peacefully, and methodically, proceeds to devour.[22] The graphic imagery helps heighten the unease that the scene is bound to incite: "His feet were immersed in a pool of boiling blood, to whose surface two or three cautious heads would suddenly rise like tapeworms from a full chamberpot [...]"[23]. Although the scene is repulsive for its anthropophagy, transgression in this instance takes on several forms. The Creator is caught in the transgressive act of eating his Creation, extinguishing it as opposed to begetting it. More significantly, He is consuming it for His own enjoyment; simply because He can. He is also exposed as a fraud, as someone who does not warrant the faith mankind has bestowed upon him. The monologue the narrator witnesses, says it all: "I have created you, so I have the right to do with you what I will. You have done nothing against me, that I do not deny. And for my pleasure, I make you suffer".[24] Ducasse subverts the significance of high and low. By po-

---

20 Lautréamont, *Maldoror*, cit., p. 64.
21 Ivi, p. 76.
22 Although there is no written proof of it, it is not unlikely that Ducasse was familiar with Goya's painting "Saturn devouring his Son" (1819–1823).
23 Lautréamont, *Maldoror*, cit., p. 76.
24 Ivi, p. 77.

sitioning Him in a scatological setting, Ducasse transgresses the accepted religious convention by allowing the divine figure to appear at His basest. Furthermore, the scene takes place as the narrator invades the Creator's privacy, voyeuristically, shattering the limits of the private, and consequently unveiling the Creator's true disposition. By defiling the figure of the one who should be worshipped for being above all, Ducasse demonstrates that the Truth mankind seeks in the presence of the Creator is not one that is worth finding.

The next example, taken from the third canto, constitutes the perfect reversal of the Great Chain of Being with the Creator firmly placed on the lowest rung.

> Everything was working out its destiny: trees, planets, sharks. All except the Creator! He was stretched out on the highway, his clothing torn. His lower lip hung down like a soporific cable. His teeth were unbrushed, and dust clogged the blond waves of his hair. [...]. He was drunk! Dreadfully drunk![25]

Not only is the Creator found in a state of drunkenness, His brazen baseness bared for all to see, but transgression manifests itself in this case when all the animals of creation one after the other kick Him in protest of their appearances and flaws. Next comes a man who defecates on the Creator for three days. The august figure of the deity is now hidden under excrement; He has become a literal pile of dung. Ducasse's transgression manifests itself in the feces; the figure of the Almighty is covered in human waste. With this image, Ducasse stresses The Creator's appropriate place in the Great Chain of Being. Not only is He on Earth, fallen from Heaven, but He has also fallen down, unable to get up, lost in an alcoholic haze. He has undergone a double fall from which He is unable to recover, forced to accept crumbs of bread from a beggar, alone and humiliated. With the images chosen, *Maldoror* presents a double perversion: on the one hand, it exploits the texts that have appeared before and on the other hand, it goes further, it pushes the limits of transgression by offering images and ideas that are bound to shake and shock even a "reader emboldened and become momentarily as fierce as what he reads".[26]

Lost in translation: perverting the original

Maldoror is a work that is similar yet different from *Les Chants de Maldoror*.[27] As David Bellos notes: "Translations are substitutes for original texts. You use them in the place of a work written in a language you cannot read with ease".[28] The fact

---

25 Ivi, p. 119.
26 Ivi, p. 27.
27 See Lautréamont, *Les Chants de Maldoror et autres textes*, Paris, Le Livre de Poche, 2001.
28 D. Bellos, *Is that a Fish in your Ear?* New York, Faber and Faber, 2011, p. 37.

that there are, to this day, few English translations of this text attests to the challenge. The act of translating, by its very nature, alters the original language, and therefore represents a form of transgression against the original work. This creates a scenario in which an original has been altered by a second author such that it could be considered a new work. In the same manner that Ducasse perverted typical linguistic custom, translation presents us with a linguistic perversion of *Les Chants de Maldoror* which creates a sort of "mise en abyme": a transgression of a transgression. Ducasse already breaks away from conventional usage of the French language by accumulating images that have no relation to each other in long sinuous sentences:

> [...] he is sixteen years and four months. He is fair as the retractility of the claws of birds of prey; or again, as the uncertainty of the muscular movements in wounds in the soft parts of the lower cervical region; or rather, as the perpetual rat-trap always reset by the trapped animal, which by itself can catch rodents indefinitely and work even when hidden under straw; and above all, as the chance meeting on a dissecting-table of a sewing-machine and an umbrella![29]

Then, by necessity, translation breaks away from the original text to make it available, as much as possible, to the English-speaking world. Translating requires the conveying of meaning. According to David Bellos, the success of a translation is not measured by its closeness to the original, but rather by how well it "works" in the target language. Since Ducasse's text can be perceived as not really "working" in the original, how can the translation be a success? How can it be made available in English while at the same time retaining the source's originalities? How can the translation allow the English-speaking reader to enjoy its idiosyncrasies and realize that they actually make sense? How can one create a transgression of a transgression? Understanding the process is necessarily an exercise in deconstruction. As Alexis Lykiard, the translator of *Les Chants de Maldoror*, affirms:

> Lautréamont's dazzling style with its wild pyrotechnics welded poetry and parody into a coherent and beautiful structure, full of sensitivity as well as strength. I hope this translation of *Les Chants de Maldoror* [...] may persuade readers to try the French text. For faced with strange puns and punctuation; with curious syntactical constructions which weave unexpected opposites into daring new patterns; with grim humour continually dissolving ecstatic lyrical flights in a cloud of ambiguous and teasing commas, a translator can only approximate.[30]

In order for a text to not only be read but enjoyed, there is a need for a certain form of "readability". There have been works of deconstruction and exercises in

---

29 Lautréamont, *Maldoror*, cit., p. 193.
30 Ivi, p. 21.

toying with the expected structure of the novel from James Joyce's *Finnegans Wake* to Julio Cortázar's *Hopscotch* to Martin Amis's *Time's Arrow* to Mark Z Danielewski's *House of Leaves*, to name a few fairly recent ones. Nevertheless, no text can survive if it is utterly unreadable. As Wolfgang Iser has demonstrated, a relationship needs to exist between the text and the reader, each doing his part for the reading experience to be fulfilled. No reader should be expected to take on the full burden of deciphering a work of fiction. Reading Ducasse is a strenuous task, one about which he warns his reader from the onset. However, Ducasse's work is readable. It constitutes a challenge and the reader must progress through the narration without falling prey to its tenaciously soporific formulations.

If the text is readable, then according to Walter Benjamin, the next question will have to deal with its translatability: "Translatability is the essential quality of certain works, which is not to say that it is essential to be translated; it means rather that a specific significance inherent in the original manifests itself in its translatability".[31] A reader familiar both with the original and the translated version will notice the challenge in translating not only the whole text and its intricacies, but maybe more importantly the title, the first element that the reader will notice. In French the heading "*Les Chants de Maldoror*" displays right away the presence of an ambiguity: are they Maldoror's cantos or cantos about Maldoror? And what exactly is a 'chant'? Are we dealing with cantos? Songs? Chants? Stanzas? By using the simple "Maldoror", Lykiard removes the ambiguity inherent to the structure but retains the one inherent to the character: the title *Maldoror* allows for the possibility that Maldoror may be the main character and/or the narrator, the possibility that the text may be for or about him and that he may be a hero, an anti-hero or none of the above. Without knowing the content of the text, the question arises as to what actually is a 'Maldoror', the capital letter allowing for the possibility that it may be a person, a place, an animal, or simply a capitalized word as titles require in the English language.

Jean Raymond claimed that *Maldoror* is a work that stands alone, situated at the cross-roads between genres, narrative points of view and exposition, transgressing these boundaries.[32] Ducasse uses the French pronoun '*on*' as one of the main components of the narration. '*On*' does not exist as such in English. It can be translated as 'one' if '*on*' is perceived as impersonal, but it may also be translated as 'I', 'you', 'we', or 'they' depending on the sentence structure and the context at hand. The French '*on*' often becomes 'you' for the English-speaking world. According to Raymond, '*on*' encompasses all the other subject pronouns,

31 W. Benjamin, *The Task of the Translator in Theories of Translation. An Anthology of Essays from Dryden to Derrida*, Chicago, The University of Chicago Press, 1992, p. 72.
32 See J. Raymond, *La Poétique du Désir : Nerval, Lautréamont, Apollinaire, Eluard*, Paris, Editions du Seuil, 1974.

incorporating the author, the reader, Maldoror and the whole of mankind.[33] If, as Jean Raymond maintains, the '*on*' is a staple of Ducasse's narration, how can this pronoun, whose comprehension can only be contextual, be translated into English, and what does the choice bring to the translated text as a whole? In the first canto, the original French passage reads: "On doit laisser pousser ses ongles pendant quinze jours"[34]. In this particular utterance, Alexis Lykiard, *Maldoror*'s translator, chose the impersonal to remain close to the original: "<u>One</u> should let one's fingernails grow for a fortnight"[35]. Later on in the same canto, the French paragraph begins with "On ne me verra pas, à mon heure dernière (j'écris ceci sur mon lit de mort) entouré de prêtres"[36]. In this case, the translator chose the passive voice to express the French '*on*': "<u>I will not be seen</u>, in my last hour (I write this on my death bed) surrounded by priests".[37] Further still, Ducasse puts forth yet another example of the '*on*': "[…] vous êtes bien sûr de voir briller la lampe, ici ou là; mais on dit qu'elle ne se montre pas à tout le monde".[38] In this case, the translator elected yet another form to express the '*on*': "[…] you are sure to see the lamp shine here and there, though <u>they say</u> it does not show itself to everyone".[39] The French '*on*' therefore, has been converted into three separate linguistic signs: 'one', the passive form, and 'they.' All convey perfectly well at least one meaning of the French passages. These few examples, however, show that translation is by definition a transgression, forcing the translator to maneuver around a simple pronoun when the '*on*' itself transgresses boundaries between subjects. Even if '*on*' is truly an essential aspect in the original work as Jean Raymond claimed, the English adaptation must, by necessity, lose that all important ambiguity as it was originally rendered. This transgression is not necessarily good or bad; it is simply a reality of the process of translation.

Transgressions of narration: undermining the act of reading

Maldoror is not the easiest text to read. It does not follow any form of linear development. There is no apparent link among the cantos except, as Gaston Bachelard argued in his *Lautréamont*,[40] the common theme of aggression. The stories that the narrator, or Maldoror, tells do not display any obvious pro-

---

33 Ivi, p. 320.
34 Lautréamont, *Les Chants de Maldoror et autres textes*, cit., p. 89.
35 Lautréamont, *Maldoror*, cit., p. 31.
36 Lautréamont, *Les Chants de Maldoror et autres textes*, cit., p. 106.
37 Lautréamont, *Maldoror*, cit., p. 43.
38 Lautréamont, *Les Chants de Maldoror et autres textes*, cit., p. 170.
39 Lautréamont, *Maldoror*, cit., p. 90.
40 See G. Bachelard, *Lautréamont*, Dallas, The Dallas Institute Publications, 1986.

gression either. They even vary in length. One constant shows Maldoror and the Creator as recurring characters throughout. The only canto that truly stands apart from the others is the sixth, which the narrator calls "a little novel of thirty pages".[41] Ducasse's style is problematic. Many critics have pondered his use of metaphors, such as the "chance meeting on a dissecting-table of a sewing-machine and an umbrella"[42] that André Breton and the Surrealists praised. As we near the end of the sixth canto, the narrator finally admits the purpose of such a tortuous narration:

> To construct mechanically the brain of a somniferous tale, it is not enough to dissect nonsense and mightily stupefy the reader's intelligence with renewed doses, so as to paralyse his faculties for the rest of his life by the infallible law of fatigue; one must, besides, with good mesmeric fluid, make it somnanbulistically impossible for him to move, against his nature forcing his eyes to cloud over at your own fixed gaze.[43]

The language in *Maldoror* is broken in various ways. The long and sinuous sentences create a feeling of dozing. The reader is hypnotized, paralyzed so as to allow the text to penetrate his/her subconscious.[44] Like a charmed snake, the reader is placed in a better position to welcome the numerous transgressions that the text offers. Additionally, Ducasse was born and raised in Montevideo. It can thus be assumed that Spanish was, before French, his native language. Some have noted in the text the presence of a few instances that sound awkward in French, attesting to Ducasse's unfamiliarity with the exact wording of the French language.[45] This potentially renders the translating process even more challenging with the end result being an English work that is problematic, in that it cannot be totally and truly accurate.

Transgression of structure deeply affects the process of reading. The act of reading is always tainted by the narrator's manipulations. In order to avoid being duped, the reader of *Maldoror* needs to work harder, pay closer attention and be more vigilant than when enjoying a lighter piece of literature. The images presented induce feelings, whether they be disgust, pleasure, curiosity, excitement, shock or fear. This forces the reader to alternate between disgust and guilty pleasure, sinning by proxy in the very act of reading as a voyeuristic occupation. Ducasse transgresses the norms in order to expose his reader to their own deepest nature:

---

41 Lautréamont, *Maldoror*, cit., p. 190.
42 Ivi, p. 193.
43 Ivi, p. 214.
44 See the works of Marcel Belanger and Laurie Edson on reading and the reader in Maldoror.
45 J. J. Lefrère's *Isidore Ducasse auteur des Chants de Maldoror par le comte de Lautréamont* is Ducasse's most comprehensive biography.

Read in one way the work will make the reader aware of appetites and desires that he never knew he had; he may not like what he finds, or he may like it too much. Reading in another way he will discover that Lautréamont delicately picks at the threads that hold his world-view together until, gently and undramatically, its fabric falls apart at the seams. But however he may choose to interpret or judge *Les Chants de Maldoror*, he may be certain of one thing; it is a work that does not leave the reader as it found him.[46]

Nothing in *Maldoror* is as a conventional text should be. The reader is forced to witness images of unbearable atrocities ensconced in a narration that is anything but traditional. *Maldoror* is a veritable collection of narratological games, endless transgressions of narratological codes. This forces the reader to take an active part in the text, questioning, wondering, remaining attentive so as not to fall in the traps the narrator claimed early on he was going to set. As Wolfgang Iser notes:

> A literary text must therefore be conceived in such a way that it will engage the reader's imagination in the task of working things out for himself, for reading is only a pleasure when it is active and creative.[47]

In *Maldoror*, the reading process is hindered on two levels: first, the narratological diversions and stylistic misdirection turn comprehension into a chaotic process. Second, once passed the linguistic challenges, one's imagination is assaulted by atrocious images. The act of reading is challenging on every page. As Michel Charles rightfully stated in his *Rhétorique de la lecture*, the dilemma with which the reader is faced at the onset of the text is not one between reading and not reading, but rather, between losing oneself and not losing oneself.[48] In so many words the narrator announces that the text is a maze, and that is up to the readership to make head or tail of it. The use of metaphors, stylistic obscurity and other syntactical peculiarities has already been studied.[49] What is interesting, in light of narratological transgressions, is the ease with which the text switches between various narrative forms, defying the reader's expectations.

Emile Benveniste defines the boundaries of the various forms for discourse and subject pronouns:

> In the first two persons, there are both a person involved and a discourse concerning that person. 'I' designates the one who speaks and at the same time implies the utterance about 'I'; in saying 'I', I cannot *not* be speaking of myself. In the second person, 'you' is

---

46 A. De Jonge, *Nightmare Culture. Lautréamont and Les Chants de Maldoror*, cit., p. 1.

47 W. Iser, *The Reading Process: A Phenomenological Approach in Reader Response from Formalism to Post-Structuralist Criticism*, Baltimore and London, The John Hopkins University Press, 1980, p. 51.

48 M. Charles, *Rhétorique de la lecture*, Paris, Seuil, 1977.

49 See in particular the works of Ora Avni, Peter W. Nesselroth, Maurice Blanchot and Gaston Bachelard.

necessarily designated by 'I' and cannot be thought of outside a situation set up by starting with 'I'; and at the same time, 'I' states something as the predicate of 'you'.[50]

Isidore Ducasse breaks these linguistic codes and toys with the language, mixing 'I', 'you' and 'he' as well as challenging their inherent status and relationship one to the other. The first-person narrative poses the first challenge, as the reader finds it difficult to locate the referent. It is unclear to whom the 'I' refers. It may be a narrator, it may be Maldoror. More often than not, the story begins with an 'I' that will later be announced as being Maldoror, but not always. It is almost impossible to form a clear image of the narrator, provided this is even the same person each time:

> "I am filthy. Lice gnaw me. Swine, when they look at me, vomit! The scabs and sores of leprosy have scaled my skin, which is coated with yellowish pus [...]".[51]

> "Each night [...] an ancient spider of the large species slowly pokes its head out of a hole [...]. It grips my throat with its legs and sucks my blood with its belly".[52]

Could these various passages describe the same narrator? Is Maldoror talking? At first, it is hard to tell. It is also difficult to determine whether the narrator/ Maldoror is asleep or awake, if he is imagining his condition or living it. The narratological ambiguity of a first-person narrative with an unclear referent increases as each account adds more narratogical transgressions. For instance, in the first canto, Edouard and his parents sit around their dining table. Their collective demeanor suddenly darkens as Maldoror approaches their abode. The text is narrated in the form of a dialogue between young Edouard and his parents. The dialogue however is also punctuated by a disturbing chorus using the first-person narrative: "I hear in the distance prolonged screams of the most poignant anguish." Is Maldoror speaking? Or is the narrator interjecting? At first glance, it is not clear who utters these recurring sentences. As Maldoror watches the family, he ponders: "What does this scene mean? There are many people less happy than these. What argument do they themselves advance for loving life? Be off, Maldoror, leave this peaceful hearth: you have no place here. He has withdrawn."[53] Once again the referent is not clear. It seems that Maldoror is talking to himself, yet "He has withdrawn" switches immediately to the first-person narrative. Could "Be off Maldoror" be perceived as a warning from the narrator? Examples of narrative ambiguity abound in the text, rendering it a challenging task to discern exactly who speaks.

---

50 E. Benveniste, *Problems in General Linguistics*, Coral Gables, University of Miami Press, 1971, p. 197.
51 Lautréamont, *Maldoror*, cit., p. 142.
52 Ivi, p. 181.
53 Ivi, p. 45.

The most provoking act of narratological transgression in *Maldoror* is conceivably the recurring use of the second person narrative. As the text progresses, the second person comes into play with the narrator/Maldoror addressing various characters directly, on three different levels. On the first level, Maldoror/the narrator often talks to himself: "Did I inadvertently crush one of its legs? Did I snatch away its youth?"[54] On the second level, Maldoror/the narrator calls out to characters, animate or inanimate, within the text such as the Ocean, the lice, and the numerous young boys that populate the text. In particular, he addressed the Creator in ways that express that character's numerous shapes: "Whoever you are, eccentric python, by what pretext do you excuse your ridiculous presence?"[55] On the third level, the narrator tries to break through the boundaries of the text, addresses the flesh and blood reader, and laments his inability to distinguish what transpires on the other side and to behold the person holding the book: "Why can I not see in these seraphic pages the face of him who is reading me? [...]. Clasp me close, and do not be afraid of hurting me".[56]

Even more troublesome are the accounts in which all three narratological forms are intertwined. In the second canto, one reads: "I grasp the quill which is going to construct the second canto…an implement ripped from the russet sea-eagle's wing …. But … what ails my fingers? As soon as I start work, their joints stay paralyzed".[57] Since there is throughout an ambiguity as to whether the text deals with Maldoror's cantos (written by him) or Maldoror's cantos (narrating his story but written by someone else) or both, at first glance it is impossible to know who the 'I' is. As the story advances, the narrator starts addressing someone directly: "Poor youth! Your face was already adequately marked by the premature wrinkles and birthmark without needing (in addition) this long sulphurous scar".[58] Who is the youth addressed here? Is the narrator talking to himself? Is an outside narrator addressing the one writing? Is Maldoror a youth? As descriptions of physical attributes are scarce at best, the ambiguity as to who is speaking and who is addressed remains. As the story unfolds, one learns that the narrator's forehead is scarred. A bandage has been applied but the blood still gushes out. Half-way through the narration a third change in perspective occurs. Maldoror (who seems to have been the 'I' after all) is mentioned in the third person: "At first sight one would not have thought Maldoror had so much blood in his arteries, for only a corpse's sheen shines on his face".[59] Is Maldoror commenting on his own condition, addressing himself as 'he'? Or are we dealing

---

54 Ivi, p. 181.
55 Ivi, p. 170.
56 Ivi, p. 175.
57 Ivi, p. 61.
58 Ibidem.
59 Ivi, p. 62.

with the subtle intrusion of an omniscient narrator commenting on Maldoror's ailment? The answer is unimportant. Disobeying the narratological codes by including them all distracts the reader from the process of reading, which constitutes the stated point of the matter.

Maldoror is a well of transgressions. From the texts that Ducasse plagiarized, exaggerated and reversed, to the images and situations portrayed, to the use of language and stylistic peculiarities, to the breaking of narratological codes and direct conversation with the narratee, transgression is not simply an inherent part of *Maldoror*, like a recurring theme or an extended metaphor. On the contrary, *Maldoror* is nothing short of pure unabated transgression.

Conclusion

Transgression is the key to understanding Ducasse' attempt at creating a new form of literature that challenged the social norms regarding morality. In *Maldoror*, transgression functions at different levels. Claiming in *Poésies* that plagiarism is necessary to the creative process, Ducasse reinvents Gothic literary masterpieces like *The Monk* by placing transgression into intertextuality as he perverts an already controversial novel. *Maldoror* plays with social and moral codes. By presenting scenes of atrocities that the Creator, the one who should be venerated, perpetrates, Ducasse breaks with morality in order to force his readership into a reevaluation of the accepted belief system. Transgression also functions in *Maldoror* as a way to question literary conventions. This intrinsic ambiguity of language turns the translation process into an unavoidable act of distortion. The reading process violates all expectations. Transgressions are an inherent element of the text, both in form and content.

Ducasse is neither the first to break literary conventions nor alone in doing so. The Marquis de Sade at the end of the eighteenth century devised scenes of insufferable perversion. Victor Hugo later wrote in his "Préface de Cromwell" (1827) that literature is best served when grotesque and sublime are used in equal measure. Hugo's stated intention was to shatter structures, change the accepted literary practices. Those who came before Ducasse usually played with either the form of their production or its content. Ducasse goes above and beyond, mixing images and blending narrative forms as he intertwines structures. Instead of eliminating some aspect of literary tradition to create something new, Ducasse chose to accumulate, to combine all genres, all narrative possibilities and all structural options to create a mosaic that functions as a whole: a collage of communicative opportunities. Scholars world-wide still read and study Ducasse. Despite the difficult imagery and the tedious narration, *Maldoror* is one of few texts that can be read through any lens. There is in *Maldoror* something for everyone. This however, could not have been possible without the abundant use of transgressions. Like Rimbaud's "long, immense et raisonné dérèglement de tous les sens" (immense, long, deliberate derangement of all the senses)[60], Ducasse has created a "long, immense raisonné dérèglement de toutes les formes" (immense, long, deliberate derangement of all the forms). Ducasse has indeed crafted a new type of literature that is nothing less than all genres, narratological codes, themes and images put together, in a great literary hodgepodge with transgression at its core.

---

60 See A. Rimbaud, *Letter of the Seer in Rimbaud, Complete Works*, Chicago, University of Chicago Press, 2005.

Paola Partenza

"Our failures are errors not crimes": The Concept of Sin in *The Nemesis of Faith* by James Anthony Froude

Introduction

The concept of sin is ambiguous and multifaceted; it implies, by definition, violation and transgression, religious precepts and secular ideas. It comprehended a wide range of characteristics and conditions in Nineteenth and Twentieth Century European cultures, from the idea of the original sin as "a crime against God that could be expiated only through death"[1] to a "subjectified abjection".[2] Its central feature, however, was traditionally offence, which brought fear and sorrow to mankind: by sinning against God, the human race was tarnished and a barrier placed between man and God.

If the Church Fathers, who became Christian intellectuals and theologians, were heirs to a long classical tradition of the effects of spirituality on man's existence, and vice versa, for centuries, they have also puzzled over and debated the topic of 'predestination' – the doctrine that God has ordained all that will happen, especially with regard to the salvation of some and not others.[3] In particular, they have argued about 'the absolute predestination of Christ', a concept associated with the teachings of St Augustine and of Calvin. Thus, both philosophers and theologians have observed, for example, that the conceptualization of sin has significant implications for those notions such as the above-mentioned predestination and free will[4]. Augustine's view marked a decisive moment in the history of Christian religion and of the subject due to his emphasis on man's self-determination. In other words, Augustine, by analysing

---

1 S. Freud, *Moses and Monotheism*, translated by Katherine Jones, New York, Vintage, 1939, p. 86.
2 J. Kristeva, *Powers of Horror. An Essay on Abjection*, translated by Léon S. Roudiez, New York, Columbia University Press, 1982, p. 128.
3 See *The Concise Oxford Dictionary of Christian Church*, ed. by E. A. Livingstone, M. W. D. Sparks, R. W. Peacocke, Oxford, Oxford University Press, 2013, p. 460.
4 Cf. J. Couenhoven, *Augustine of Hippo*, in *The Routledge Companion to Free Will*, ed. by Kevin Timpe, Meghan Griffith, Neil Levy, New York and London, Routledge, 2017, p. 247. Here Couenhoven refers to Augustine's *City of God*.

men's behaviour, provided the theological resources to interpret their fall, as Jesse Couenhoven notes: "There are many times when God simply allows us to do as we please. Adam and Eve's fall from innocent perfection into sin is the prime but not the sole example of such situation, where God foreknew a thing that God did not cause".[5] This conviction does not much differ from that which has been passed down over the centuries.

Nineteenth-century scholars have seen an exponential increase of interest in theological explanations concerning the relation between sin and the subject's will, where sin becomes a notion related mainly to will. This idea has provided a model for describing the subject's relation to the world and to himself, creating, in turn, a connection between freedom and human nature whose root sense provides a foundation for their theoretical or theological exegesis. To a large extent, different interpretations of the issue rely on the subject's understanding of the sort of meaning believers or unbelievers employ[6].

There is no question that religion had a profound impact on Victorian private and public lives, and it is undeniable that certain themes were central to different kinds of works. Thoughts on the relationship between human beings and God are also seen in literature. Specifically, the conflict between religious precepts and free will led few authors to believe that sin is an immoral act, placing emphasis on man's most damaging emotions, such as doubt, guilt and fear contained within the story of the Fall. As Jeffrey von Arx observes, the Victorian crisis of faith, however,

> [I]s shaped by the literature of conversion and reverse conversion: autobiographical accounts like Newman's *Apologia,* barely concealed autobiography like Froude's *Nemesis of Faith,* or novels of conversion like Mrs Humphry Ward's *Robert Elsmere.*[7]

Scholars who have focused on James Anthony Froude's work have recognised *The Nemesis of Faith* (1849) as one of the most problematic novels of the time due to the controversial questions it deals with, and, nowadays, is little analysed. Despite the work being burnt in the refectory at Exeter College, it was reprinted many times,[8] although in 1880 Froude "told his friend John Skelton he would not

---

5 Ivi, p. 252.

6 One interesting piece is *The Novel and Other Discourses of Suspended Disbelief,* by C. Gallagher and S. Greenblatt, in *Practicing New Historicism,* Chicago, Chicago University Press, 2000, pp. 163–210.

7 J. von Arx, *The Victorian Crisis of Faith as Crisis of Vocation,* in *Victorian Faith in Crisis: Essays on Continuity and Change in Nineteenth-Century Religious Belief,* ed. by R. J. Helmstadter and B. Lightman, Stanford, Stanford University Press, 1990, p. 262.

8 Cf. C. Brady, *Emboldening the Weak: The Early Fiction of James Anthony Froude,* in *Victorian Fiction Beyond the Canon,* ed. by Da. Downes and T. Ferguson, London, Palgrave Macmillan, 2016, p. 45.

allow it to be republished during his lifetime".[9] After the publication of *Nemesis* there was a "dust storm", as Froude called it, and the work was defined as "a sketch of the author's own mind, a *manual of infidelity*".[10]

Notwithstanding, opinions on the book varied widely, and on September 1849, a reviewer wrote in the *Spectator:* "This remarkable book is an emancipation of that deep thought on the condition of man and the conventions of society [...]".[11] Froude's descriptions have often proved to be open to philosophical and theological investigation. Perhaps these inquiries are capable of responding sensitively to his representations whose qualities were clearly stated in *Fraser's Magazine* the same year,

> The most striking quality in Mr Froude's writing is his descriptive eloquence. His characters are all living before us, and have no sameness. His quickness of eye is manifest equally in his insight into human minds, and in his perceptions of natural beauty [...].[12]

The pronouncement of the future George Eliot may be taken as typical: "We are sure that its author is a bright particular star, though he sometimes leaves us in doubt whether he be not a fallen 'son of the morning'".[13]

For commentators, Froude's scandalous novel provided fairly simple matter by which to represent their dissension, and his most conservative contemporaries did not conceal their disagreement with the author. The resulting Victorian criticism detected mostly the amoral powers of the *Nemesis of Faith*, with its concern for righteous conduct. By contrast, this essay will attempt to show that the novel offers an accurate analysis of both moral and theological universes in which the concept of sin, as it has been emphasised by the author, is a complex web of doubts from which man cannot escape; hence sin is merely the result of man's freedom.

"This faithless age". Provocative perspectives

In *The Nemesis of Faith*, Froude provides a variety of provocative perspectives and constant speculations on the miserable human condition, writing: "[It] had been but a cry of pain"[14]. In the *Preface's* opening passage, he is prone to define

---

9 Letter to Skelton, 19 March 1880, qtd. in C. Brady, *James Anthony Froude. An Intellectual Biography of a Victorian Prophet*, Oxford, Oxford University Press, 2013, p. 113.

10 Cf. J. Markus, *J. Anthony Froude. The Last Undiscovered Great Victorian*, New York and London, Scribner, 2005, p. 42. See also W. H. Dunn, *James Anthony Froude: A Biography 1818-1856*, Oxford, Oxford at the Clarendon Press, 1961.

11 *The Spectator*, qtd. in J. A. Froude, *The Nemesis of Faith*, cit., p. 229.

12 *Fraser's Magazine*, Id., p. 229.

13 J. Markus, cit., p. 45.

14 W. H. Dunn, *Froude*, I, cit., p. 148.

"the moral of human life" by emphasising that it "is never simple, and the moral of a story which aims only at being true to human life cannot be expected to be any more so" (*Preface* to *NF*, p. iii). Despite the work being defined as heretical, and its author accused of blasphemy and apostasy,[15] we might argue that it is a theologically challenging work, since it shows the crisis of a man who is desperately trying to answer to his own doubt and loss of faith,[16] and who also poses the question of sin in terms of doubt and freedom.[17]

Since the beginning, the author announces his intention to look through and behind the "historic Christianity"[18] in order to glimpse the origin of the process of its controversy.[19] He affirms, indeed, that "Religion of late years has been so much a matter of word controversy, it has suffered so complete a divorce from life, that life is the last place in which we look for it".[20] Froude sees this detachment from life as making religion a matter of reliability, it clashes with his age: "Times are changed", he observes. "This age is an age of fact – it believes only in experience – it is jealous and inquiring" (*Preface* to *NF*, p. x).

Thus, in the *Preface* Froude focuses on "the wrenching religious doubts of an entire generation"[21] as they emerge from his depiction of Markham Sutherland (the protagonist), a fictional character who has much in common with the autobiographical voice that materialises from the lines of the novel:

> It is this struggle which I have painted in the history of Markham Sutherland; a struggle which, as it seemed to me, his conscience forced upon him – which the tenderness of his nature made more painful than it would have been to a person with less in him of material of good – and out of which he only escaped with his moral insight distorted, and with his spiritual constitution too shattered to enable him to face successfully the trials of life (*Preface* to *NF*, p. v).

---

15 See D. Cook, *Froude's Post-Christian Apostate and the Uneven Development of Unbelief*, "Religion and Literature", Vol. 38, N. 2 (Summer, 2006), pp. 49–71.

16 See R. Ashton, *Doubting Clerics. From James Anthony Froude to Robert Elsmere via George Eliot*, in Jasper and Wright, *The Critical Spirit and the Will to Believe*, New York, St. Martins, 1989.

17 Interesting here is B. Willey, *More Nineteenth Century Studies: A Group of Honest Doubters*, London, Chatto and Windus, 1963; see also E. Duffy, *Saints, Sacrilege and Sendition: Religion and Conflict in the Tudor Reformations*, London, Berlin, New York, Sidney, Bloomsbury, 2012.

18 M. Cowling, *Religion and Public Doctrine in Modern England*: Volume 3: Accommodations, Cambridge, Cambridge University Press, 2004, p. 14.

19 As R. Black notes, "[...] Christianity needed only suitable reinterpretation to be seen as profoundly true", *Moral Scepticism and Inductive Scepticism* in "Proceedings of the Aristotelian Society", New Series, Vol. 90 (1989–1990), pp. 65–82, p. 68.

20 J. A. Froude, *The Nemesis of Faith*, Preface to 2nd edition, London, John Chapman, 1849, p. iii. All in-text references to the *Preface* (hereafter, *Preface* to *NF*) are to this edition.

21 J. Markus, cit., p. 2. See also *The Science of History in Victorian Britain: Making the Past Speak*, by I. Hesketh, London and New York, Routledge, 2011 and P. Partenza, *Dynamics of Desacralization. Disenchanted Literary Talents*, Göttingen, V&R unipress, 2015, pp. 71–90.

This epistolary novel[22] represents a reflection on the complex system of moral norms in action and explores its implications for the character involved. The work centres around a quest of identity and true religious calling, as Sutherland stresses: "Before I can be made a clergyman, I must declare that I unfeignedly believe all 'the canonical writings of the Old Testament;' and I cannot" (*Preface* to *NF*, p.10). One might read these words with the secure conviction that this expression composes the nucleus of Sutherland's confession. But, in Froude's intention, the work's main focus is the dichotomy between the external constraint to which the character is subject (moral impulse) and free will. Sutherland feels the responsibility for his double motivation, which is compounded by his own personal failure to reach "conclusions [which are] unanswerable" (*Preface* to *NF*, p. viii).

Froude's carefully structured work is supported by a broad acquaintance with philosophy and theology.[23] It begins with a colloquial résumé of Markham Sutherland's life to his friend Arthur; he does appear to offer an illustration of his present situation and his deep anxiety about his father's will, as he asserts:

> My father is very anxious to see me settled into some profession or other, [...] I am not a genius, and I cannot trust myself to hope I should be an expectation, and so I go round and round, and I always end where I began, in difficulties (pp. 2–3).[24]

At the beginning of the novel Sutherland is a silhouette, a flat character. He gains depth as he begins to reflect on himself, his life, random objects around him and, of course, on Church and religion ("[...] at least the Church is open to you, you will say, and that is what my father says", *NF*, p. 5). As he progresses in thoughtfulness and self-awareness, he eventually involves himself in doubts about religion, though at a high point in this questioning he wonders, with some anxiety causing intense bewilderment and psychological confusion: "What possible reason can I have for not taking orders?" (*NF*, p. 9).

Commentators have observed that the novel appears, since the first letters, as the contemplation of a man who poses the question of religion without redundancy or artificial hiddenness, but it is perfectly inserted into the debate of the time.[25] Daniel Cook, for instance, considers the novel "a response to ra-

---

22 The first part of *The Nemesis of Faith* takes the traditional structure of the epistolary or letter writing form, in which, as J. Herman points out: "the binary opposition between literary discourse and reality is replaced by a semiotic triad: literary discourse, authentic discourse and reality", qtd. in Th. O. Beebee, *Epistolary Fiction in Europe, 1500–1850*, Cambridge, Cambridge University Press, 1999, p. 8.

23 Froude was indebted to both classical and modern philosophy, but he mainly followed and analysed the works of Spinoza, whose system of thought had a profound influence on him.

24 J. A. Froude, *The Nemesis of Faith*, London, John Chapman, 1849, pp. 2–3. All in-text references to *The Nemesis of Faith* (hereafter, *NF*) are to this edition.

25 Cf. E. Deeds Ermarth, *The English Novel in History 1840–1895*, London, Routledge, 1997, p. 43.

tionalist models of secularisation, but even more obviously a reply to the Car-
lylean model of spiritual development".[26] Actually, when Sutherland explains, for
instance, the metaphysical *difficulties* in believing that "the Psalms and
Prophecies were composed under the dictation of the Holy Spirit" he justifies his
thought, saying:

> If there were no difficulties but these, only my reason were perplexed, I could easily
> school my reason; I could tell myself that God accommodated His revelations to the
> existing condition of mankind, and wrote in their language. But, Arthur, bear with me,
> and at least hear me; though my head may deceive me, my heart cannot. I will not, I must
> not, believe that the all-just, all-merciful, all-good God can be such a Being as I find him
> there [the Old Testament] described. He! He! to have created mankind liable to fall – to
> have laid them in the way of a temptation under which He knew they would fall, and then
> curse them and all who were to come of them, and all the world, for their sakes; jealous,
> passionate, capricious, revengeful, punishing children for their fathers' sins, tempting
> men, or at least permitting them to be tempted into blindness and folly, and then
> destroying them. Oh, Arthur, Arthur! this is not a Being to whom I could teach poor
> man to look up to out of his sufferings in love and hope (*NF,* pp. 10–11).

In trying to determine God's attitude toward mankind, Sutherland highlights
that the God of the Old Testament leads humanity in a wrong direction in
interpreting His words, and, moreover, God seems to express indifference to
man's fall or towards the descendants who pay "for their fathers' sins". Sutherland's words show that the divine presence is not for man's salvation; God
looks at the fall of man without sorrow but with indignation, and this is one of the
reasons why he cannot believe in "such a Being". Herein Sutherland creates an
alleged ambivalence about the Divine Creator since God loves human beings,
but, at the same time, He (God) believes it right that they be punished for all
transgressions and sins that have changed human destiny. Sutherland seeks to
show that God makes no attempt to reveal His love of mankind, and to doubt that
God approves of its destruction would be to imply that He is not the merciful God
who is prone to save them. Thus, the character's intense despair is caused by his
meditation on human beings who

> [a]re thrown out into life, into an atmosphere impregnated with temptation, with
> characters unformed, with imperfect natures out of which to form them, under ne-
> cessity of a thousand false steps, and yet with every one scored down for vengeance;
> [...] and this under the decree of an all-just, all-beautiful God – the God of love and
> mercy (*NF,* p. 15).

These words reveal the novel's central tenet, that of human limits and im-
perfection, along with the perception of a self-contradictory God of mercy. While
not wishing to deny God's paternal love, Sutherland's words are no less striking

---

26 D. Cook, cit. p. 51.

for how they raise the possibility that God could bring about a radically different outcome: He would destroy an order of which He is the ultimate guarantor. Of the same tenor is Sutherland's reflection when he posits:

> [I]f I am to be a minister of religion, I must teach the poor people that they have a Father in heaven, not a tyrant; one who loves them all beyond power of heart to conceive; who is sorry when they do wrong, not angry; whom they are to love and dread, not with caitiff coward fear, but with deepest awe and reverence, as the all-pure, all-good, all-holy (*NF*, p. 17).

"A Father in heaven", Sutherland writes, aspiring to a Father who is inclined to forgive and not to punish. In the passages above, Sutherland seems to allude to and criticise a kind of isomorphism not only between the actions of the divine and humans, but also between their methods of determining justice. At the same time, he feels prone to consider Christianity the best expression of God's love, when a *man* appears in mortal guise and is recognised by his disciples. The divine strategy for defeating sin, evil and death is fulfilled in Christ's suffering love. Thus, Sutherland emphasises that,

> [t]o save his [Christ] example, to give reality to his sufferings, he was a man nevertheless. In him, as philosophy came in to incorporate the first imagination, was the fulness of humanity as well as the fulness of the Godhead. [...] the religion of Christ ended with his life, and left us instead but the Christian religion (*NF*, p. 87).

"A thorny road". Sutherland's growing doubt

Sutherland's doubts and perplexities towards the Christian doctrine is highlighted when he considers the issue of mankind's reward and punishment, as we have already seen, particularly their relation to the will of God. In Letter X, the narrator intentionally reflects and deploys a standard conception of God's will by stating,

> I believe God is a just God, rewarding and punishing us exactly as we act well or ill. [...] But a doctrine out of which, with our reason, our feeling, our logic, I at least can gather any practical instruction for mankind [...] such a doctrine I cannot find it (*NF*, pp. 69, 72).

On the one hand, Sutherland's scepticism[27] seems based on the lack of practicality of the doctrine's principles. On the other, he realises that the stability of the religious apparatus of the Victorian world seems based more on a system of

---

27 On this aspect see A. Gabbey, '*A Disease Incurable*': *Scepticism and the Cambridge Platonists*, in *Scepticism and Irreligion in the Seventeenth and Eighteenth Centuries*, ed. by R. H. Popkin and A. Vanderjagt, New York, E. J. Brill, 1993, pp. 71–91.

norms that derive their authority from those societies, such as "The Bible Society", or "religious tea-parties", which are engaged to preserve and reinforce the
social role of religion, rather than an authentic religious feeling. Sutherland
makes no attempt to conceal his dislike, noting that he "didn't marry any of them
– that was the first great sin. [He] patronised no societies and, [he] threw cold
water on philanthropy schemes" (*NF,* p. 58); that is, he refused to associate
himself with "the meaningless rituals and distorted priorities of his fellow Anglican clergymen".[28] All this illustrates how Sutherland's doubts manifest
through a series of inquiries, speculations and situations that he is not able to
overcome. Thus, he emerges as a sceptic,[29] a "cool observer of religion, a detached Christian, always rational and a free-thinker".[30] Among the many questions he poses, Sutherland's insistent thought is focused on the Creation, examining the most important aspects of it, and he reflects on and asks himself
about the position of humanity within it, a humanity that has the weight of sin
upon itself; he realises that he is not able to answer his questions, but rather can
only underline that traditions and precepts are inadequate. They try to explain
the nature of the universe, of life, while admitting that Creation itself is the one
unknowable mystery. In *Shadows of the Clouds*[31] for example, the protagonist,
Canon Fowler, states,

> But at present there are many mistakes which science has failed to understand, and one
> is obliged to make them to know they are mistaken; one must fall to know what it is to
> stand [...] to be obliged so many times to be taught, and taught the same thing over and
> over; each time forgetting the meaning of the word, and having to look it out again in
> the dictionary of suffering.[32]

Like Fowler, Sutherland is haunted by the broader anxieties and frustrations of
his times. To make clear his suffered position, he confesses his profound in-
quietude and growing doubt to the bishop, Mr Hickman, who, at the end, with "a
voice of mournful kindness" says: "It is a terrible trial. Only He who is pleased to
send such temptation can give you strength to bear it" (*NF,* p. 74). What is
interesting is that it appears that here a long-silenced problem is coming to light:

---

28 S. Stark, *A 'Monstrous Book' After All? James Anthony Froude and the Reception of Goethe's
    Die Wahlverwandtschaften in Nineteenth-Century Britain*, "The Modern Language Review",
    Vol. 98, n. 1 (Jan. 2003), pp. 102–116, p. 108.
29 See R. M. Blake, *A Criticism of Scepticism and Relativism*, in "The Journal of Philosophy",
    Vol. 21, N. 10 (May 1924), pp. 253–272; and J. Annas, J. Barnes, *The Modes of Scepticism*,
    Cambridge, Cambridge University Press, 1985.
30 Cf. A. M. Cameron, *The "Scepticism" of Procopius*, "Historia: Zeitschrift für Alte Geschichte",
    Bd. 15, H. 4 (Nov. 1966), pp. 466–482, p. 466.
31 *Shadows of the Clouds,* first published in 1847 under the pseudonym Zeta, "caused a brief
    furore in the Oxford popular press" as C. Brady notes in his Emboldening the Weak, cit.,
    p. 45.
32 Zeta, (pseudonym of J. A. Froude), *Shadows of the Clouds*, London, John Ollivier, 1847, p. 117.

that is, God is both source and patron of human self-determinations. To let man eat from the tree of knowledge ("The tree of knowledge, that death in life". *NF*, p. 26) has given him the freedom to doubt, to sin, and to choose between two alternatives,[33] as Sutherland affirms: "[...] we can say a power lay in the individual will of choosing either of two courses – in other words, to discover sin" (*NF*, p. 92).

The character's considerable doubt allows him to admit anything is possible. The problem is, however, that such radical scepticism involves contradictions, deriving from his critical examination of precepts, actions, religions, and philosophies, so that he seems to incline sometimes towards rationalism, and sometimes towards a form of convinced religiosity and belief. In actual fact, Sutherland shows alternatively his pessimistic resignation or a lively religious afflatus, yet a consideration of his remarks reveals he is pious rather than doubtful. This is seen at the beginning of the novel when Sutherland records without any sign of disbelief that "this universe, and every smallest portion of it, exactly *fulfils the purpose* for which the Almighty God designed it"; that is, he is firmly convinced that Creation is the result of God's will; yet then he changes his opinion, and he does not recognise Creation and humankind as a priority. Rather, he considers only humanity, and in particular man as "a real man, [who] can live and act manfully in this world, not in the strength of opinions, not according to what he thinks, but according to what he *is*" (*NF*, p. ix).

Thus, despite Sutherland expressing his bewilderment, and despite his attitude towards religion revealing the limitations and dangers of his decision (not to take orders) – in Mr Hickman's words – he ultimately feels "again free, again happy" as he declares, because "all the poor and paltry net-work in which [he] was entangled, the weak intrigues which like the flies in the summer irritate far worse than more serious evils, [he has] escaped them all" (*NF*, p. 76). Sutherland's sense of freedom resides in his own choice. This reflection leads to the assumption that man's actions are the result of a challenge[34]: man's freedom *versus* man's responsibility. Consequently, free will, as an instrument of measuring man's responsibility, equates freedom with the making of correct decisions, a pattern that clarifies how human decisions establish norms of conduct in relation to both the social and religious spheres. In this perspective, the concept of sin has to be correctly understood and interpreted. As Sutherland points out:

> The source of all superstition is the fear of having offended God, the sense of something within ourselves which we call sin. Sin, in its popular and therefore most substantial sense, means the having done something to gratify ourselves which we knew, or might

---

33 R. Trigg, *Sin and Freedom*, in "Religious Studies", Vol. 20, N. 2 (Jun., 1984), pp. 191–202, p. 191.

34 Cf. Ivi, p. 192.

have known, was displeasing to God. It depends, therefore, for its essence on the doer having had the power of acting otherwise than he did. When there is no such power there is no sin. [...] In reflecting upon our own actions we find that they arise from the *determination of our will*, as we call the ultimate moral principle of action, upon some object. When we will, we will something not nothing. [...] And in every action, if analysed, the will is found to have been determined by the presence of the greatest degree of desirableness on the side of towards which it has been determined (*NF*, p. 90, italics mine).

The philosophical attitude the character shows leads to a consideration that the core of the question resides in the individual will, in the humans' ability to choose what is good. Such a position draws a parallel between seduction and desirableness of the object; therefore, human action is submitted to attraction and self-gratification. Speculation on this aspect of man's actions is the response of man's reason when his experience confronts moral principles. In this way, Sutherland's critical analysis exposes the flaws of moral and religious convictions when he talks about "the determination of our will" and of "man's action" instead of God's will. He seems to denote the limits of man's process of salvation by implicitly denouncing that man absolves himself by affirming that we now live in a creation damaged by human sin as equivalent of will. "When there is no such power there is no sin" he says. However, what Sutherland does not understand is why "a man of two goods should choose the lesser, knowing it *at the time* to be the lesser. [...] at the time of action" (*NF*, p. 91). Less articulated than they are supposed to be, "the nearness or distance of objects may alter their relative magnitude, or appetite or passion may obscure the reflecting power, and give a temporary impulsive force to a particular side of our nature" (*NF*, p. 91). Appetite and passion represent the essential dimension of man's moral depth in which the manifestation of self-consciousness begins. And, according to Froude, man's capacity to resist the tempting appetites is the precondition for a pristine moral individual who exemplifies the power of human resolve, perseverance, and faith.

Analysis of sin reckons with the presence of the man's will "of choosing either of two courses", and action in the primordial time. Froude asserts that,

Actions are governed by motives. The power of motives depends on character, and character on the original faculties and the training which they have received from *men* or *things* among which they have been bred. Sin, therefore, as commonly understood, is a chimera (*NF*, p. 92, Froude's italics).

He, however, rejects the doctrine of original sin and replaces it with an original "unreflecting state" that is "the state of innocence" (*NF*, pp. 93–94). Thus, Froude's speculation extends to the origin of man and his Fall, and his thought moves within the medium of religion, of myth, and of philosophy which serve to explain his own position and his scepticism. He acknowledges "the perfection of man's nature; [...]" and, at the same time, he seems to absolve man by stating that "Our failures are errors not crimes – nature's discipline with which God teaches us; [...]" (*NF*, p. 96). In other words, the narrator exploits the idea that there is a power beyond man's will and action, something that is in relation either to natural order or dependent on God, but more importantly he devaluates *sin*, defining it as *error*, not crime. His vision, however, is essentially anthropological; that is, Sutherland shows human beings as equipped with an anthropological conscience and moral reasoning powers which reinforce their free will. In terms of concept and ideology, Sutherland, according to Ciaran Brady, agrees with Feuerbach when he maintains that "mankind's concept of sin is a reflection of the state of its cultural advance, from primitive fears to the metaphysical philosophers' proof that no force antagonistic to God could exist, [...]".[35] It is interesting to see that this is exactly the same attitude as Froude himself adopts, although Sutherland's position has been defined by scholars as "inchoate, fragmentary, and private".[36]

Until now, the novel has emphasised the formative role of man's will. And, according to Froude, it is misleading to interpret man's free will as if it were incompatible with religion and God. In his opinion the distortion stems from a false view of sin, divine justice, and punishment, which assume that because human beings are not perfect moral exemplars they cannot enforce basic issues of right and wrong. The goal of the doubting process is to arrive at such beliefs that are certain and indubitably true; through Sutherland's confessional biography the author aspires to make clear his idea of faith and religion conveying the notion of a possible harmony of the two worlds.

"Confessions of a Sceptic"[37]. Markham Sutherland's relativist position

Sutherland's "relativist position"[38] brought him into the realm of doubt and uncertainty, including doubts on the cogency of the concept of sin. Many critics have read a story of personal torment in Froude's work, a religious odyssey. Brady, for instance, sees in Sutherland's *Confessions of a Sceptic* "a partial au-

---

35 C. Brady, cit., p. 151.

36 Ivi, p. 150.

37 *Confessions of a Sceptic* is the title with which the author opens the second part of the novel. It is indicative of the novel's progression and of the protagonist's growing intellectual and religious dilemmas.

38 C. Brady, cit., p. 150. See also, Ch. Herbert, *Victorian Relativity. Radical Thought and Scientific Discovery*, Chicago and London, The University of Chicago Press, 2001.

tobiography within a partial biography"[39], then stresses that "immediately the narrative turns to an intensely nostalgic recall of the halcyon days of Sutherland's childhood".[40] As we have seen, Froude devotes attention to depicting a character as a man who "believes that the true foundations of religious faith lie 'in this early unreasoning reverence [...] not in authenticities, and evidences and miracles'".[41] There are many elements of nostalgia and melancholy in Froude's writing, and their presence provokes an unmistakably nostalgic mood in *The Nemesis of Faith*. Nevertheless, the novel is a dynamic rethinking of classical and modern philosophies and theories, vividly expressed and full of psychological intensity and emotion. Like many of his other works, *The Nemesis of Faith* is a self-referential novel. Froude depicts the inner world of the character by means of meticulous analysis of his own thoughts, passion and intuition, through which he aspires to achieve a closer intimacy with his readers. The author, by virtue of Sutherland, proceeds with exhibiting a certain temper or disposition of mind, a hesitancy to believe and tendency to doubt; thus, even in the second part of the novel, Sutherland appears as an alienated figure who expresses disillusionment with his own search for religious truth. Consequently, in the *Confessions of a Sceptic,* the character continues to pose many questions and few easy answers, making his position more problematic and controversial: it is nominally oriented towards the flaws of religion and the social and moral problems the protagonist, through his assay, raises.

Among the theological issues focused by Sutherland, two of these have a philosophic/religious significance: the idea of desire and desirableness, which have led to a broader meaning of the concepts of sin and guilt. Indeed, Froude's focus on "the ethics of love and sexual attraction"[42] becomes fundamental for his speculation, and, in the second part of his work, they have become inextricably intertwined. Their provenance seems to be clear: yes, from Froude's friends at Oxford, Arnold and Clough, but mainly from Goethe of *Elective Affinities*[43] who had great influence on his conjectures on love and desire.

Once more the author examines the problem of sin by means of layers such as unfaithful love, desire, and sense of guilt, all treated as ethical issues. What we finally have is wrapped in uncertainties and caveats; tensions, feelings and questions abound in the author's head: he captures and transmits to the reader

---

39 C. Brady, cit., p. 151.
40 Ibidem.
41 Ibidem and *The Nemesis of Faith,* cit., p. 117.
42 C. Brady, cit., p. 153.
43 See in particular R. L. Wolf, *Gains and Losses: Novels of Faith and Doubt in Victorian England*, New York, Garland Pub, 1977; K. Tillotson, *Novels of the 1840s,* Oxford, Oxford University Press, 1956, and G. P. Landow (ed.) *Approaches to Victorian Autobiography*, Athens, Ohio University Press, 1979.

the sense of uncertainty Sutherland lives, pointing out that even doubting God's existence, man is not free from his guilt, as only a reaffirmation of values and morality can lead to a return to ethics, that is, to moral correctness of specified conduct.[44] In other words, Sutherland carries the ache and anxiety that was transmitted to him intergenerationally.

In order to raise these ethical questions, Froude involves readers, disclosing to them the protagonist's adulterous living situation. In fact, Sutherland is involved in an adulterous love affair with Helen Leonard, a married and unloved woman. The lovers devote themselves to each other, but when Annie, Helen's daughter, dies, Sutherland's guilt leads him to attempt suicide. He is saved by Frederick Mornington, his tutor at Oxford, who convinces Sutherland to convert to Catholicism and devote his life to religion by entering a monastery. But the plot leads to a fatal end, a tragic destiny which the character cannot avoid: because of his religious doubts, he abandons the monastery and "dies for want of a will to live",[45] as Ciaran Brady states out. Such a condition has brought him to perceive a raised moral weakness and confusion that have worsened his profound sense of guilt. Sutherland does not always admit to being a sinner, but deep down inside, he recognises that he is, carrying the awareness that he has sinned or is sinning. Unlike Sutherland, Helen does not consider her love for him a crime, rather believing that her marriage without love was her true sin that has brought her only to be unaware of her situation. This is the reason why she wants to explain her intimate condition to her husband in order to obtain sympathy and release: "I will throw myself at his feet, and ask his forgiveness; not for loving you [Sutherland], but for ever having been his. That was my sin; to promise I knew not what, and what I could not fulfil" (*NF*, pp. 187–88).

Although Helen's logic in explaining her reasons is beyond moral and social comprehension ("If we have broken this world's laws, and must die, then love will give us strength" *NF*, p. 188), she knows that society itself demands dishonour and amoral conduct be punished, a formula that appears as the archetypal pattern of the novels' moral paradigm of the Victorian Age. Notwithstanding, she is convinced that her daughter's death is not a punishment for her adultery, but rather for having married a man without love. Despite Helen's awareness of the moral and religious code rigorously condemning adultery on the part of a woman, she persists in affirming her conviction, "that her sin had been in her marriage, not in her love" (*NF*, p. 225) for Sutherland. The character's identity to a great extent determines her motivations and actions. Helen hereby absolves herself of all responsibility and blame. Even though she does not reconcile herself

---

44 See S. Pihlström, *Transcendental Guilt: On an Emotional Condition of Moral Experience*, in "The Journal of Religious Ethics", Vol. 35, N. 1 (Mar., 2007), pp. 87–111.

45 C. Brady, cit., p. 154.

with either the dogma or the Church, at the end of the novel, she dies happy: "it was a hard trial to the weeping sisters who hung around her departure to see with what serene tranquillity the unpardoned sinner, as they deemed her, could pass away to God" (*NF*, p. 226). At this point, the author appears much more sympathetic to the cause of freedom and will than was the public opinion expressed after the publication of the novel. Froude's decision to include in the novel a sense of *justice* – that is, pity with Helen's misfortunes – emerges as one of the elements which operate within a larger moral framework that extends throughout the novel and the universe it creates.

If Sutherland's responsibility compounds Helen's errors, his personal failure consists of his "moral and psychological immaturity".[46] Sutherland can feel his emotions surge as his inner thoughts manifested feelings of remorse, regret, sadness, and guilt. Moreover, he feels responsible for Helen's destruction; he is convinced to have brought disgrace on her. However, Sutherland's own conduct emerges as particularly blameworthy "[...] not for what he had done, but for what he had not done" (*NF*, p. 226). He thinks that he is paying for his disloyalty, doubts and fear, showing a disjunction between his perspective and that of Helen. The original *offence* – to question Christian religion, to deny either God or Scripture,[47] and to have an amoral conduct – is re-enacted within the novel. The pattern of sin and punishment concludes with a sense of *apparent divine justice*[48] extending over generations: "amidst the wasted ruins of his life [...] no living being was left behind him upon earth, who would not mourn over the day which brought life to Markham Sutherland" (*NF*, pp. 226–27).

Conclusion

> Markham's new faith fabric had been reared upon the clouds of sudden violent feeling, and no air castle was ever of more unabiding growth; doubt soon sapped it [...] (*NF*, p. 226).

Thus Markham Sutherland enforces his past; the author makes the reader conscious that the character's strenuous efforts to answer to his own dilemma have not permitted easy solutions.

Froude, as we have seen, has been concerned in various ways with the exploration of some aspects of the moral and theological universe described in *The Nemesis of Faith*. The author has mainly sought to investigate the connection between human action, sin and human responsibility, which the work seems to

---

46 Ivi, p. 155.
47 Cf. D. Cook, cit., p. 60.
48 Interesting is S. Pihlström, cit., pp. 87–111.

have deployed, all issues that are found throughout the quality of *argumentation* offered in support of the character's introspective self-analysis. Thus, although Sutherland eventually presents himself as merely the agent of secular reading of religious precepts, and he shows to be very keen to enquire into the issues which have impacted social and cultural structures of his age, his personal involvement and his choice of confessional biography are more than a matter of conveniently available materials. It is an opportunity to scrutinise religious precepts, philosophies and their coherence in practical life. Additionally, the extensive discussion of the character shows that Sutherland's view of the religious world, and the spiritual meditations included in his writings to Arthur – which depart from theological and philosophical pieces – define the author's propensity for analysis that raises questions and challenges to the traditional view of the age. Thus, if the first part of the novel has been that of the common view of religion as peculiarly moralistic, in the second part, the author's subversive ambition has led him to discuss human actions, man's will, responsibility and punishment from a human point of view. Froude's lens makes his subject look more courageous than that presented by the theological universe of the Scriptures, and certainly no less significative.

To conclude, the pattern of belief/unbelief, to which the idea of sin is connected, dominates the novel. However, the continuity of religious thought is illustrated by Sutherland's anxiety and sceptical worries; he appears as an inquiring lone figure withdrawn into himself and contemplating his life. He is not able to reconcile himself to a religious world that has provided more doubts than certainties. Like the character, "[...] the text is unable to reconcile itself to a world in which even sacred language is unsteady, perhaps (in De Man's sense) tropological, a world in which intellectual choices are not just difficult but in some sense illusory [...]" as Cook notes.[49] Sutherland's speculations and actions seem to conform to a radically different moral world, distant from the Christian theological tradition. Yet, both morality and theology underlie the novel, despite the word nemesis indicating the attitude of God towards "human beings who have broken the moral and spiritual code".[50] Sutherland's reason, together with that of his creator Froude, does not draw him closer to God, but he continues to be a convinced advocate of man's self-determination.

---

49 Ibidem.
50 Redfield J. M., *Nature and Culture in the Iliad. The Tragedy of Hector*, Expanded Edition, Durham and London, Duke University Press, 1994, pp 115 ff. The Greek word nemesis (νέμεσις) means "distribution of what is due" (Liddell-Scott-Jones); but in Froude's context might be significant Thomas Merton's definition: "*memesis* – [is] *a fatal retribution in which man's power becomes his own destruction*", in *The Literary Essays of Thomas Merton*, ed. by P. Hart, New York, New Directions Books, 1981, p. 258.

Notes on Contributors

Igor Djordjevic is the Chair of the Department of English and an Associate Professor of Early Modern Literature at Glendon College, York University, the author of *Holinshed's Nation: Ideals, Memory, and Practical Policy in the* Chronicles, and *King John (Mis)Remembered: The Dunmow Chronicle, the Lord Admiral's Men, and the Formation of Cultural Memory.* His research interests are in the history of reading and the relationship between English cultural memory and the various forms of and approaches to historical writing in the early modern period.

Margarete Rubik is Emerita Professor of English Literature at the University of Vienna, Austria. Her research interests range from Restoration and eighteenth-century literature to the nineteenth-century novel and modern drama. She has published widely in these fields, including a study on *Early Women Dramatists 1550 to 1800*, an edition of the works of Delarivier Manley and Eliza Haywood (*Eighteenth Century Women Playwrights*, Vol. 1) and edited volumes on *Aphra Behn and her Female Successors*, on *Revisiting and Reinterpreting Aphra Behn*, and a special issue of *Women's Writing* on Aphra Behn. She has also compiled several collections of essays, for instance on *Intertextual and Intermedial Re-writings of Jane Eyre*, on *Stories of Empire*, and on *Staging Interculturality*. She is now in the process of editing Behn's posthumous play *The Younger Brother* for Cambridge University Press.

John Maune is a professor in the Hokusei Gakuen University Junior College English Department, Sapporo, Japan, where he teaches content-based courses in both biology and literature. He has given presentations at conferences for literature, education, human evolution, and language teaching on a wide-variety of topics ranging from Mind, Brain, and Education teaching hacks, the carnivalesque in *Coriolanus*, to human nature in *Romeo and Juliet*. He will chair a seminar at the Northeast Modern Language Association annual conference (NeMLA 2018) on Shakespeare's source materials.

Ibrahim A. El-Hussari is a Professor of English and Cultural Studies at the Departments of English and Humanities, School of Arts and Sciences of the Lebanese American University, Beirut, Lebanon. He is a holder of a Ph.D degree in Literature from the University of Leicester, UK. His teaching load is focused on teaching Rhetoric, Comparative Literature and Cultural Studies at both undergraduate and graduate levels. Besides, he organizes international academic conferences and the annual poetry symposium for poet Jawdat Haydar at LAU, Beirut. His field of research interest includes inter-cultural communication, discourse analysis, comparative literature, and translation. He has participated in many International Conferences around the world and written extensively on a variety of topics related to his field of interest. He has so far published five academic books, translated twenty one story books for children and young adults, and published forty four articles in international, peer-reviewed journals as well as several chapters in special-issue volumes. He is also a research reviewer and an active member on many university journal boards, namely ATINER (Greece), GLOSSA (USA), CEJISS (Czech Republic), IRJAH (Pakistan) and IADA (Spain).

Eloïse Sureau-Hale is Associate Professor of French at the Department of Modern Languages, Literatures and Cultures at Butler University in Indianapolis, Indiana. She has publihed numerous articles and book chapters such as "Traces, Doubles et Panoptique. Le rôle du regard dans *Le Comte de Monte Cristo* d'Alexandre Dumas." (2012); "*Les Chants de Maldoror:* Plaisir de la négation, négation du plaisir" (2009); "Spectres, monstres et fantômes. *Les Chants de Maldoror* et le spectacle de la fantasmagorie" (2008); "Isidore Ducasse précurseur d'Odilon Redon. L'hypotypose en noir et blanc" (2008) (with Stamos Metzidakis); "Un voyage de l'œil à l'autre ou Maldoror traverse le miroir. Quelques remarques sur l'identité et le flou dans *Les Chants de Maldoror*" (2006); "Gothic Film in the Classroom: exploring examples of British, German, French and American Gothic literature with filmic springboard" (with Fred Yaniga) Cambridge Scholars Publishing (2011); and translations: Kostroun, Daniella, Eloïse Sureau (translator) "La Mère Louise-Anastasie Dumesnil et Mlle de Joncoux, dernières gardiennes de la réforme de Port-Royal" in *Ruine et Survie de Port-Royal. Chroniques de Port-Royal* (2012); Thompson, William, Eloïse Sureau (translator) "Baudelaire et l'étudiant américain", *Bulletin Baudelairien* (1999).

Renu Josan is Professor at the Department of English Studies, Dayalbagh Educational Institute, Deemed University, Agra-5, India. Her research interests include Indian English Literature, Mystic Literature, Feminist Studies, Translation of Work from Hindi into English. She has published many articles such as "Oppression to Assertion: Dalit Consciousness in Om Prakah Valmiki's Joothan"

(USA, 2012); "Community of Women: Feminist Articulations in the Poems of Emily Dickinson and Adrienne Rich" (*Atlantic Critical Review* 2011). Authored a book titled "Poetic Vision of Emily Dickinson and Adrienne Rich". She has presented research papers in national and international conferences and published research articles in national and international journals. My areas of research include mystic literature, literature of the marginalised, eco poetry, Indian English literature. She is the academic member of the Athens Institute for Education and Research and on the Reviewer's Board of Athens Journal of Philology.

Paola Partenza is Associate Professor at the University of Chieti-Pescara, Italy, Department of Modern Languages, Literatures and Cultures, University "G. d'Annunzio", where she teaches several courses of English Literature. She published a volume on Tennyson's poetry (2002[1], 2012), on female writings, (2008), and on Jane Austen: (2015). She is Editor-in-Chief with Andrea Mariani of the the the book series *Passages – Transitions – Intersections* (Göttingen: Vandenhoeck & Ruprecht), and she has edited *Dynamics of Desacralization. Disenchanted Literary Talents*, (V & R unipress Göttingen, 2015). She is *peer reviewer* for several international journals. She is the author of essays in collections and journals. Among the many novelists and poets to whom she has devoted essays are William Godwin, Mary Hays, Mary Wollstonecraft, Jane Austen, Elizabeth Gaskell, Alfred Tennyson, T. S. Eliot, Shakespeare, Andrew Marvell and Rebecca Harding Davies and P.D. James. Her research interests include Eighteenth-Century Literature and Culture; Nineteenth-Century Literature and Culture; Jane Austen; Female Writings; Victorian Poetry; the connection between Literature and Religion, and Science and Literature. She is the academic member of the Athens Institute for Education and Research; she is a member of ANDA and The Tennyson Society.

Bibliography

Achinstein, S. *Milton and King Charles, in The Royal Image: Representations of Charles I*, ed. by T. N. Corns, Cambridge, Cambridge University Press, 1999.

Anderson, T. P. *Performing Early Modern Trauma from Shakespeare to Milton*, Burlington, Ashgate, 2006, pp. 178–180.

Annas, J. Barnes, J. *The Modes of Scepticism*, Cambridege, Cambridge University Press, 1985.

Ashton, R. *Doubting Clerics. From James Anthony Froude to Robert Elsmere via George Eliot*, in Jasper and Wright, *The Critical Spirit and the Will to Believe*, New York, St. Martins, 1989.

Barton, A. *Essays, Mainly Shakespearean*, Cambridge, Cambridge University Press, 1994.

Beebee, O. Th. *Epistolary Fiction in Europe, 1500-1850*, Cambridge, Cambridge University Press, 1999.

Behn, A. *A Pindaric Poem to the Reverend Doctor Burnet, on the Honour he did me of Enquiring after me and my Muse*, in *The Works of Aphra Behn*, ed. by J. Todd, Vol. 1, London, Pickering, 1992, pp. 307–310.

- *To The Unknown Daphnis on his Excellent Translation of Lucretius*, in *The Works of Aphra Behn*, ed. by J. Todd, Vol. 1, London, Pickering, 1992, pp. 25–28.

- *The Golden Age in The Works of Aphra Behn*, ed. by J. Todd, Vol. 1, London, Pickering, 1992, pp. 30–35.

- *A Paraphrase on the Lords Prayer*, in *The Works of Aphra Behn*, ed. by J. Todd, Vol. 1, London, Pickering, 1992, pp. 171–174.

- *Love Letters Between a Nobleman and His Sister*, in *The Works of Aphra Behn*, ed. by J. Todd, Vol. 2, London, Pickering, 1993.

- *The History of the Nun*, in *The Works of Aphra Behn*, ed. by J. Todd, Vol. 2, London, Pickering, 1993, pp. 205–258.

- *Oroonoko*, in *The Works of Aphra Behn*, ed. by J. Todd, Vol. 3, London: Pickering, 1995, pp. 51–119.

- *Lycidus*, in *TheWorks of Aphra Behn*, ed. by J. Todd, Vol. 4, London, Pickering, 1993, pp. 377–421.

- *The Rover*, in *The Works of Aphra Behn*, ed. by J. Todd, Vol. 5, London, Pickering, 1996, pp. 445–521.

- *The Dutch Lover*, in *The Works of Aphra Behn*, ed. by J. Todd, Vol. 5, London, Pickering, 1996, pp. 157–238.

- *Sir Patient Fancy*, in *The Works of Aphra Behn*, ed. by J. Todd, Vol. 5, London, Pickering, 1996, pp. 1–81.
- *The Feign'd Curtizans*, in *The Works of Aphra Behn*, ed. by J. Todd, Vol. 6, London, Pickering 1996.
- *The Roundheads*, in *The Works of Aphra Behn*, ed. by J. Todd, Vol. 6, London, Pickering, 1996.
- *The Emperor of the Moon*, in *The Works of Aphra Behn*, ed. by J. Todd, Vol. 7, London, Pickering, 1996.
- *The Widdow Ranter*, in *The Works of Aphra Behn*, ed. by J. Todd, Vol. 7, London, Pickering, 1996.
- *The Younger Brother*, in *The Works of Aphra Behn*, ed. by J. Todd, Vol. 7, London, Pickering, 1996.
- *The City Heiress*, in *The Works of Aphra Behn*, ed. by J. Todd, Vol. 7, London, Pickering, 1996.
- *The Luckey Chance*, in *Works*, ed. by J. Todd, Vol. 7, London, Pickering, 1996, pp. 209–284.
- (*Epilogue* to), *The Widow Ranter*, in *the Works of Aphra Behn*, ed. by J. Todd, Vol. 7, London, Pickering, 1996.

Bellos, D. *Is that a Fish in your Ear?* New York, Faber and Faber, 2011.

Benjamin, W. *The Task of the Translator in Theories of Translation. An Anthology of Essays from Dryden to Derrida*, Chicago, The University of Chicago Press, 1992.

Benveniste, E. *Problems in General Linguistics*, Coral Gables, University of Miami Press, 1971.

Berthoud, J. *Joseph Conrad: The Major Phase*, Cambridge, Cambridge University Press, 1979.

Biondi, G. F. *An History of the Civil Wars of England between the Two Houses of Lancaster and York*, trans. by H. Carey Earl of Monmouth, London, 1641.

Black, R. *Moral Scepticism and Inductive Scepticism*, in "Proceedings of the Aristotelian Society", New Series, Vol. 90 (1989–1990), pp. 65–82.

Blake, R. M. *A Criticism of Scepticism and Relativism*, in "The Journal of Philosophy", Vol. 21, N. 10 (May 1924), pp. 253–272.

Bower, T. *Sacred Violence in Marvell's Horatian Ode*, in "Renascence: Essays on Values in Literature", LII, 1999.

Bowers, F. (ed.), *The Complete Works of Christopher Marlowe*, vol. II, Cambridge, Cambridge University Press, 1981.

Bradley, A.C. *Shakespearean Tragedy: Lectures on Hamlet, Othello, King Lear, Macbeth*, 2nd edn., London, Macmillan, 1905.

Brady, C. *James Anthony Froude. An Intellectual Biography of a Victorian Prophet*, Oxford, Oxford University Press, 2013.

- *Emboldening the Weak: The Early Fiction of James Anthony Froude* in *Victorian Fiction Beyond the Canon*, ed. by D. Downes and T. Ferguson, London, Palgrave Macmillan, 2016.

Budra, P. A Mirror for Magistrates and the De Casibus Tradition, Toronto, University of Toronto Press, 2000.

Burke, E. *A Philosophical Enquiry in to the Origins of our Ideas of the Sublime and Beautiful*, Oxford, Oxford University Press, 1990.

Cable L. *Milton's Iconoclastic Truth*, in *Politics, Poetics, and Hermeneutics in Milton's Prose*, ed. by D. Loewenstein and J. G. Turner, Cambridge, Cambridge University Press, 1990.

Cameron, A. M. *The "Scepticism" of Procopius* "Historia: Zeitschrift für Alte Geschichte", Bd. 15, H. 4 (Nov. 1966), pp. 466–482, p. 466.

Campbell, L. B. (ed.), *The Mirror for Magistrates*, Cambridge, Cambridge University, Press, 1938.

Camus, A. *The Rebel: an Essay on Man in Revolt*, New York, Vintage Books, 1991.

Charles, M. *Rhétorique de la lecture*, Paris, Seuil, 1977.

Charney, M. *Shakespeare's Roman Plays: The Function of Imagery in the Drama*, Cambridge, Harvard University Press, 1963.

Chernaik, W. *Sexual Freedom in Restoration Literature*, Cambridge, Cambridge University Press, 1995.

– *The Myth of Rome in Shakespeare and His Contemporaries,* Cambridge, Cambridge University Press, 2011.

Coleridge, S. T. 'The Rime of the AncientMariner', in Rewey Inglis/Donald Stauffer (eds.): *Adventures in English Literature*, New York, Harcourt, Brace, 1952.

Collier, J. *A Short View of the Immorality and Prophaneness of the English Stage* (1698). com/plays/corio_1_2.html.

Conrad, J. *Heart of Darkness*, London, Penguin, 1973.

Cook, D. *Froude's Post-Christian Apostate and the Uneven Development of Unbelief,* "Religion and Literature", Vol. 38, N. 2 (Summer, 2006), pp. 49–71.

Cook, J. *Shakespeare's Players*, 2nd edn., London, Harrap Limited, 1985.

Couenhoven, J. *Augustine of Hippo*, in *The Routledge Companion to Free Will*, ed. by Kevin Timpe, Meghan Griffith, Neil Levy, New York and London, Routledge, 2017.

Cowling, M. *Religion and Public Doctrine in Modern England:* Volume 3: Accommodations, Cambridge, Cambridge University Press, 2004.

Cressy, D. *Remembrancers of the Revolution: Histories and Historiographies of the 1640s*, in "Huntington Library Quarterly", LXVIII, 2005.

Crew, F. *The Sin of the Fathers: Hawthorne's Psychological Themes*, London, OUP, 1996.

Curry, J. *Shakespeare on Stage*, London, Nick Hern Books, 2010.

Daems, J. , Nelson H. F. (eds.) *Eikon Basilike with Selections from Eikonoklastes by John Milton*, Peterborough, ON, 2006.

Daniel, S. *The Civil Wars Between the Houses of Lancaster and York*, ed. by L. Michel, New Haven, Yale University Press, 1958.

Davenport, R. *King John and Matilda*, sig. I2v (London, 1655).

De Jonge, A. *Nightmare Culture. Lautréamont and Les Chants de Maldoror*, New York, St. Martin's Press, 1973.

Deeds Ermarth, E. *The English Novel in History 1840-1895*, London, Routledge, 1997.

Djordjevic, I. *Holinshed's Nation: Ideals, Memory, and Practical Policy in the Chronicles*, Burlington, Ashgate, 2010.

– *King John (Mis)Remembered: The Dunmow Chronicle the Lord Admiral's Men, and the Formation of Cultural Memory*, Burlington, Ashgate, 2015.

– *"No chronicle records his fellow": Reading Perkin Warbeck in the Early Seventeenth Century*, in "Renaissance and Reformation", XL.2, 2017, pp. 63–102.

Dollimore, J. *Radical Tragedy*, Chicago, University of Chicago Press, 1984.

Duffy, E. *Saints, Sacrilege and Sendition: Religion and Conflict in the Tudor Reformations*, London, Berlin, New York, Sidney, Bloomsbury, 2012.

Dunn, W. H. *James Anthony Froude: A Biography 1818-1856*, Oxford, Oxford at the Clarendon Press, 1961.

Egan, J. *Oratory and Animadversion: Rhetorical Signatures in Milton's Pamphlets of 1649*, in "Rhetorica", XXVII, 2009, pp. 189-217.

Elyot, Sir T. *The Boke Named the Governour*, London, 1531.

Empson, W. *Seven Types of Ambiguity*, New York, New Directions, 1947.

Etherege, G. *The Man of Mode*, ed. by J. Barnard, London, A&C Black 1988 [1979].

Fenton, Sir G. *A Forme of Christian Pollicie*, London, 1574.

Filmer, (Sir) R., *Patriarcha*, London, 1680.

Fischlin D., Fortier M. (eds.), *James I, The True Law of Free Monarchies and Basilikon Doron*, Toronto, Centre for Reformation and Renaissance Studies, 1996.

Ford, J. *The Chronicle History of Perkin Warbeck: A Strange Truth*, ed. by P. Ure, London, Methuen, 1968.

Fowler, J. M. *Should We Ever Judge Others?* "Dialogue", 11 (2 1999), 28.

Freud, S. *Civilization and Its Discontents*, James Strachey (trans.), London, Norton, 1930/ trans., 1961.

– *Moses and Monotheism*, transl. by Katherine Jones, New York, Vintage, 1939.

Froude, J. A. *The Nemesis of Faith*, Preface to 2nd edition, London, John Chapman, 1849.

Gabbey, A. '*A Disease Incurable*': *Scepticism and the Cambridge Platonists* in *Scepticism and Irreligion in the Seventeenth and Eighteenth Centuries*, ed. by R. H. Popkin and A. Vanderjagt, New York, E. J. Brill, 1993, pp. 71-91.

Gallagher C., Greenblatt, S. (eds.), *The Novel and Other Discourses of Suspended Disbelief*, in *Practicing New Historicism*, Chicago, Chicago University Press, 2000, pp. 163-210.

Garganigo, A. *Mourning the Headless Body Politic: the Regicide Elegies and Marvell's* "Horatian Ode", in "Exemplaria", XV, 2003, pp. 509-550.

Genette, G. *Palimpsestes*, Paris, Seuil, 1982.

Glanvill, J. *Seasonable Reflections* (1676), in Spurr, J. *The manner of English Blasphemy, 1676-2008, in Religion, Identity and Conflict in Britain: From the Restoration to the Twentieth Century, Essays in Honour of Keith Robbins*, ed. by S. J. Brown, F. Knight and J.Morgan-Guy, London/New York, Routledge, 2016 [2013].

Goddard, H.C. *The Meaning of Shakespeare*, vol. 2. 2nd edn., Chicago, University of Chicago Press, 1960.

Golding, W. *Lord of the Flies*, London, Noble & Barnes, 1954.

Greenblatt, S. *Renaissance Self-Fashioning: From More to Shakespeare*, Chicago, University of Chicago Press, 1980.

– *Will in the World*, 2005, available at: www.norton & co.

Guerard, A. J. *Conrad the Novelist*, Boston, Harvard University Press 1958.

Hart, P. (ed.) *The Literary Essays of Thomas Merton*, New York, New Directions Books, 1981.

Hawthorne, N. *The Scarlet Letter*, Hertfordshire,Wordsworth Editions Limited, 1999.

– *The Scarlet Letter*, Boston, Ticknor & Fields, 1850.

Haywood, E. *Love in Excess, or, The Fatal Enquiry*, ed. by D. Oakleaf, Peterborough, ON, Broadview, 2000^2.

Helgerson, R. *Milton Reads the King's Book: Print, Performance, and the Making of a Bourgeois Idol*, in "Criticism", XXIX, 1987, pp. 1–25.

Herman, J. *Le Mensonge romanesque: parametres pour l'etude du roman épistolaire en France*, Leuven, Leuven University Press, and Amsterdam, Rodopi, 1989, in Th. O. Beebee, *Epistolary Fiction in Europe*, 1500–1850, Cambridge, Cambridge University Press, 1999.

Hesketh, I. *The Science of History in Victorian Britain: Making the Past Speak*, London and New York, Routledge, 2011.

Hobbes, T. *Leviathan* [1651], ch. XII, http://www.gutenberg.org/files/3207/3207-h/3207-h. htm#link2HCH0013.

Hooton, H. *A Bridle for the Tongue* (1709), in Spurr, J. *The manner of English Blasphemy, 1676–2008, in Religion, Identity and Conflict in Britain: From the Restoration to the Twentieth Century, Essays in Honour of Keith Robbins*, ed. by S. J. Brown, F. Knight and J.Morgan-Guy, London/New York, Routledge, 2016 [2013].

Horacius Flaccus, Q. *Carmina* I. 11. http://www.thelatinlibrary.com/horace/carm1.shtml.

Hunt, M. *The Backward Voice of Coriol-anus*, in "Shakespeare Studies", 32, 2004, pp. 220–239.

Iser, W. *The Reading Process: A Phenomenological Approach in Reader Response from Formalism to Post-Structuralist Criticism*, Baltimore and London, The John Hopkins University Press, 1980.

Jacobs, N. *Robbing His Captive Shepherdess: Princess Elizabeth, John Milton, and the Memory of Charles I in the Eikon Basilike and Eikonoklastes*, in "Criticism", LIV, 2012.

Kingsley-Smith, J. *Cupid in Early Modern Literature and Culture*, Cambridge, Cambridge University Press, 2010.

Knowles, R. *Shakespeare's Arguments with History*, New York, Palgrave, 2002.

Kristeva, J. *Powers of Horror. An Essay on Abjection*, transl. by Léon S. Roudiez, New York, Columbia University Press, 1982.

Lacey, A. *The Cult of King Charles theMartyr*, Woodbridge, UK, Boydell Press, 2003.

Landow, G. P. (ed.), *Approaches to Victorian Autobiography*, Athens, Ohio University Press, 1979.

Laskovsky, H. *Blurring Images in Heart of Darkness*, in G. Deyan, *A World of Lies in Heart of Darkness*, "Journal of Language Teaching and Research", Vol. 2, N. 4, pp. 763–768, July 2011.

Lautréamont, *Les Chants de Maldoror et autres textes*, Paris, Le Livre de Poche, 2001.

– *Les Chants de Maldoror*, Engl. Trans. *Maldoror and the Complete Works of Comte de Lautréamont*. Cambridge, Exact Change, 2011.

Leggatt, A. *Shakespeare's Political Drama*, London, Routledge, 1988.

– A. *Shakespeare's Political Drama: The History Plays and the Roman Plays*, New York, Routledge, 1988.

Lewis, M. *TheMonk*, London, Penguin, 1998.

Lewis, W. *The Lion and the Fox*, London, Grant Richards, 1927.

Livingstone, E. A., Sparks, M. W. D., Peacocke, R. W. (eds.), *The Concise Oxford Dictionary of Christian Church*, Oxford, Oxford University Press, 2013.

MacCallum, M.W. *Shakespeare's Roman Plays and Their Background*, New York, Russell and Russell, 1967.

Markus, J. J. *Anthony Froude. The Last Undiscovered Great Victorian*, New York and London, Scribner, 2005.

Marvell, A. "An Horatian Ode upon Cromwell's Return from Ireland", in *The Poems of Andrew Marvell*, ed. by Nigel Smith, Harlow, UK, Pearson Education Limited, 2007.

Mathiessen, F. O. *American Renaissance*, Delhi, OUP, 1973.

Maune, J. *Revealing Tells, Bawdy and Otherwise, in Coriolanus*, in "Athens Journal of Humanities and Arts X Y", 2016, pp. 1–15.

– *Topsy-Turvy and Other Carnivalesque Aspects in Coriolanus*, in "Athens Journal of Philology", 2016, pp. 23–38, available from: http://www.athensjournals.gr/philology/2016-3-1-2-Maune.pdf.

McClay, W.M. *The Strange Persistence of Guilt*, in "THE HEDGEHOG REVIEW", Spring 2017/19, 1.

McDowell, P. *The Women of Grub Street. Press, Politics and Gender in the London Literary Marketplace 1678–1730*, Oxford, Clarendon Press, 1998.

McDowell, N. *Milton, the Eikon Basilike, and Pamela's Prayer: Re-Visiting the Evidence*, in "Milton Quarterly", XLVIII, 2014, pp. 225–226.

McKnight, L. B. *Crucifixion or Apocalypse?: Refiguring the Eikon Basilike*, in *Religion, Literature, and Politics in Post-Reformation England, 1540–1688*, ed. by D. B. Hamilton and R. Strier, Cambridge, Cambridge University Press, 1996, pp. 138–160.

Miles, R. *The 1790s: the effulgence of Gothic in The Cambridge Companion to Gothic Fiction*, Cambridge, Cambridge University Press, 2002.

Millington, R. H. (ed.), *The Cambridge Companion to Nathaniel Hawthorne*, Cambridge, CUP, 2004.

Nietzsche, F. *The Genealogy of Morals*, 2016, available at: www.gutenberg.org/ebooks/52319.

Ovidius Naso, P. *Ars Amoria* I. 16. http://www.poetryintranslation.com/PITBR/Latin/ArtofLoveBkI.htm.

Partenza, P. *Dynamics of Desacralization. Disenchanted Literary Talents*, Göttingen, V & R unipress, 2015.

Pihlström, S. *Trascendental Guilt: On an Emotional Condition of Moral Experience*, in "The Journal of Religious Ethics", Vol. 35, N. 1 (Mar., 2007), pp. 87–111.

Ravelhofer, B. *News Drama: the Tragic Subject of Charles I*, in *English Historical Drama, 1500–1600*, ed. by T. Grant and B. Ravelhofer, New York, Palgrave Macmillan, 2008, pp. 179–180.

Raymond, J. *La Poétique du Désir : Nerval, Lautréamont, Apollinaire*, Eluard, Paris, Editions du Seuil, 1974.

Redfield J. M., *Nature and Culture in the Iliad. The Tragedy of Hector*, Expanded Edition, Durham and London, Duke University Press, 1994.

Rimbaud, A. *Letter of the Seer in Rimbaud, Complete Works*, Chicago, University of Chicago Press, 2005.

Rivers, I. *Reason, Grace, and Sentiment. A Study of the Language of Religion and Ethics in England, 1660–1780. Vol. 2: Shaftesbury to Hume*, Cambridge, Cambridge University Press, 2000.

Routledge Encyclopedia on Philosophy, version 1.0: 2002, London, Routledge.

Scharnhorst, G. *The Critical Response to Nathaniel Hawthorne's The Scarlet Letter*, Westport, Greenwood Press, 1992.

Shakespeare, W. *Coriolanus*, K. Deighton, (ed.), London, Macmillan, 1900, available from: http://www.shakespeare-online.com.

Sharpe, K. *Image Wars: Promoting Kings and Commonwealths in England, 1603-1660*, New Haven, Yale University Press, 2010.

– *The Royal Image: An Afterword, in The Royal Image: Representations of Charles I*, ed. by T. N. Corns, Cambridge, Cambridge University Press, 1999.

Shore, D. *"Fit though Few": Eikonoklastes and the Rhetoric of Audience*, in "Milton Studies", XLV, 2006, pp. 129-148.

Skerpan Wheeler, E. *Eikon Basilike and the Rhetoric of Self-Presentation*, in *The Royal Image: Representations of Charles I*, ed. by T. N. Corns, Cambridge, Cambridge University Press, 1999, pp. 135-136.

Skerpan, E. P. *Rhetorical Genres and the Eikon Basilike*, in "Explorations in Renaissance Culture", XI, 1985, pp. 99-111.

Southcombe, G. and Tapsell, G. *Restoration Politics, Religion, and Culture. Britain and Ireland 1660-1714*, London, Palmgrave Macmillan, 2010.

Spurr, J. *The manner of English Blasphemy, 1676-2008, in Religion, Identity and Conflict in Britain: From the Restoration to the Twentieth Century, Essays in Honour of Keith Robbins*, ed. by S. J. Brown, F. Knight and J. Morgan-Guy, London/New York, Routledge 2016 [2013].

Stark, S. *A 'Monstrous Book' After All? James Anthony Froude and the Reception of Goethe's Die Wahlverwandtschaften in Nineteenth-Century Britain*, "The Modern Language Review", Vol. 98, n. 1 (Jan. 2003), pp. 102-116.

Stevens, P. *Milton, Drama, and the Nation, in The Elizabethan Theatre XV*, ed. by C. E. McGee and A. L. Magnusson, Toronto, Meany, 2002, pp. 320-321.

– *Milton's Janus-Faced Nationalism: Soliloquy, Subject, and the Modern Nation State*, in "Journal of English and Germanic Philology", C, 2001, pp. 247-268.

Strohm, P. *York's Paper Crown: Bare Life and Shakespeare's First Tragedy*, in "Journal of Medieval and Early Modern Studies", XXXVI, 2006, pp. 75-101.

Tillotson, K. *Novels of the 1840s*, Oxford, Oxford University Press, 1956.

Tilmouth, C. *Passion's Triumph over Reason: A History of the Moral Imagination from Spenser to Rochester*, Oxford, Oxford University Press, 2007.

Todd, J. *The Secret Life of Aphra Behn*, London, Andre Deutsch, 1996.

Trigg, R. *Sin and Freedom*, in "Religious Studies", Vol. 20, N. 2 (Jun., 1984), pp. 191-202.

Turner, A. *Nathaniel Hawthorne: An Introduction and Interpretation*, New York, Holt, Rineheart, and Winston, 1961.

VanSpanckeren, K. *Outline of American Literature (M)*, USA, The US Information Agency, 1994.

Von Arx, J. *The Victorian Crisis of Faith as Crisis of Vocation* in *Victorian Faith in Crisis: Essays on Continuity and Change in Nineteenth-Century Religious Belief*, ed. by R. J. Helmstadter and B. Lightman, Stanford, Stanford University Press, 1990.

Wells, S., Taylor, G., et al. (eds.) *The Oxford Shakespeare: The Complete Works*, Oxford, Clarendon Press, 2005.

White, G. E. *Ministry of Healing*, Idaho, Pacific Press Association, 1942.

Wilcher, R. *What Was the King's Book for?: the Evolution of Eikon Basilike*, in "The Yearbook of English Studies", XXI, 1991, pp. 218-228.

Willey, B. *More Nineteenth Century Studies: A Group of Honest Doubters*, London, Chatto and Windus, 1963.

Williamson, M. L. *Raising their Voices. British Women Writers, 1650–1750*, Detroit, Wayne State University Press, 1990.

Wolf, R. L. *Gains and Losses: Novels of Faith and Doubt in Victorian England*, New York, Garland Pub, 1977.

Zagorin, P. *Cudworth and Hobbes on Is and Ought, in Philosophy, Science and Religion in England 1640–1700*, ed. by R.Kroll, R. Ashcraft, P. Zagorin, Cambridge, Cambridge University Press 1992, pp. 128–148.

Zaller, R. *Breaking the Vessels: The Desacralization of Monarchy in Early Modern England*, in "The Sixteenth Century Journal", XXIX, 1998, pp. 757–778.

Zeta, (pseudonym of J. A. Froude), *Shadows of the Clouds*, London, John Ollivier, 1847.

Index of Names

Passages – Transitions – Intersections

Paola Partenza, Andrea Mariani (eds.)

Volume 4: Alessandro Giovannucci

Perspectives historico-esthétiques dans l'œuvre de Fernando Liuzzi

2018. 118 Seiten, paperback
€ 25,– D
ISBN 978-3-8471-0841-2

Volume 3: Greta Colombani

A gordian shape of dazzling hue

Serpent Symbolism in Keats's Poetry

2017. 126 Seiten, paperback
€ 25,– D
ISBN 978-3-8471-0775-0

Volume 2: Andrea Mariani

Italian Music in Dakota

The Function of European Musical Theater in U.S. Culture

2017. 250 Seiten, paperback
€ 35,– D
ISBN 978-3-8471-0655-5

Volume 1: Paola Partenza (ed.)

Dynamics of Desacralization

Disenchanted Literary Talents

2015. 179 Seiten, paperback
€ 35,– D
ISBN 978-3-8471-0386-8

V&R Academic

Verlagsgruppe Vandenhoeck & Ruprecht | V&R unipress

www.v-r.de